Experiences

Norman Verl Stones

Illustrations by Dwight Nacaytuna

Order this book online at www.trafford.com
or email orders@trafford.com

Most Trafford titles are also available at major online book retailers.

Printed in the United States of America.

ISBN: 978-1-4907-2621-2 (sc)
       978-1-4907-2622-9 (e)

Library of Congress Control Number: 2014901766

Our mission is to efficiently provide the world's finest, most comprehensive book publishing service, enabling every author to experience success. To find out how to publish your book, your way, and have it available worldwide, visit us online at www.trafford.com

Any people depicted in stock imagery provided by Thinkstock are models, and such images are being used for illustrative purposes only.
Certain stock imagery © Thinkstock.

Trafford rev. 01/29/2014

Trafford
PUBLISHING® www.trafford.com
North America & international
toll-free: 1 888 232 4444 (USA & Canada)
fax: 812 355 4082

Contents

Subject

Introduction

Since retirement I have had more time to contemplate my life. I watched how things changed for my grandparents and parents. The use of automobiles, radio and telephone and electrical distribution was important. I thought it would be good to share this knowledge with my grand children. I would not have an opportunity to sit down with them and share my experiences. Things have changed faster each generation it seems.

There is not much time left perhaps and one thing I have is memories. Some may not be accurate but as I lay in bed at night before I go to sleep, it is pleasant to recall things that impacted my life. Some things were not so good but you learn from those also.

This could be the impetus for them to do something similar for their grand children. I am sure there will be many changes that they witness. It was tough back then and it will be tough in other ways in the coming generations.

Making myself sit and put it down in black and white is the harder part. Thanks to computers and software and my having taken typing in high school and later having a job that required a lot of keyboard work is the easier part.

Birth

I was born on a farm in a house that was built by my great grandfather about 1880. It was in north central Kansas just a few miles from the geographical center of the continental United States. Very soon after I was born, there was a loud noise that startled my aunt Ruby who was helping my mother. She thought I had fallen out of bed, but a book had been knocked off onto the floor. Some time later as I was being given a bath, my grandmother Mary Alice Francis Stones said, "Oh look at him stretch! He is going to be tall." I did reach six foot as an adult so she was right. These are stories that I was told over and over as I grew up.

The farm is 2 ½ miles west of Kansas State Route 281. The roads all run north and south or east and west and were dirt surfaced. After rains or melting snow they were slick and muddy and during dry weather dusty and bumpy. It is about 10 miles north to the small town of Red Cloud, Nebraska and about the same south to Lebanon, Kansas. There was no electricity or running water.

The house was built on a hill a hundred yards or so from the road. It had a covered back porch with a large hinged floor that had steps down into the cellar that had a dirt floor and walls. At the east end was a wall that had a door that led into the basement with a wood floor and walls. The east wall was limestone blocks about one foot thick and two feet long. A door and two windows looked out onto a porch of wood. Above the basement was the living room, two bedrooms and the front porch with a railing all the way around. The back porch led into the kitchen. There was a large pantry and a long storage room. The milk separator was in the pantry. The coal and wood fired (Majestic) cook stove was on the east side of the kitchen. On the end of the stove was the reservoir where water heated when the stove was hot. A wash stand was on the south wall where the water bucket sat with a dipper to get a drink or put water in the wash pan to wash up. Two cabinets and a round tale with chairs and a small table where the radio and batteries were placed completed the furnishings. We were one of the last families to get a radio. It was a Philco and a man came and ran an antenna from the house to the windmill so we would have good reception. High on the south wall 8-penny nails were located to hang coats. There were no closets in the house. Once, when a cousin was visiting, we were running back and forth from the kitchen to the living room. As I chased him he pushed the door and it bounced off of the clothes and swung half closed. I ran headlong into it and received a huge bump on my forehead.

Just east of the house was the pig-pen that was fenced and had several low buildings to protect the sows when they had baby pigs in early spring. There was a vee shaped trough to put in soaked corn to feed the hogs. Pigs are thought to be dirty. They head for the mud during hot weather to keep cool as they don't have the sweat glands like other animals. They have one area where they all go to the bathroom. Other animals and chickens go anywhere they happen to be

West of the house across a small draw was the chicken house with wood slats for the birds to roost on and boxes on the east end with straw where the hens laid their egg every day. On the west end was a two-hole shed for our bathroom. There were a couple of low buildings just to the south.

South of the house was the wind mill with a small milk house and two large water tanks for stock to drink from. The mill was manufactured by the Aermotor company. Another popular make was the Dempster company. . It is fortunate that the wind blows almost all the time in Kansas as pumping by hand is very labor intensive. The well was about 50 feet deep and never ran dry even during the dust bowl years of the 1930s.

Beyond that was a granary building with an attached sloped roof addition that was used as a garage. On further south was the barn with east side being a place to shelter cattle in the winter. The west side had stalls with containers to hold hay and oats. There were also two small storage units for storing grain and the corn-sheller. Nails were on the wall to hang the harness for the horses. The upstairs or haymow was open for hay to be piled for winter when it snowed and the livestock could no longer graze. On further south was the garden when we raised potatoes, sweet corn, radishes, onions, tomatoes and other vegetables. It was far enough away to keep the chickens from tearing up plants.

Barbed wire fences were around the whole farm. There were about 100 acres in pasture and the rest in cultivation. This was my world as I grew up. I had no brothers and my sister didn't make her entrance until I was 13 and living in town going to high school. It was about 1/8 of a mile west to one cousin. It was about ¼ of a mile east on the north side of the road where another cousin lived. We lived on the homestead and they lived on the timber claim that my Great Grandfather James Timothy Stones had procured under the Homestead Act.

Mastoid Operation

It was in the spring and I was running barefoot through the plowed ground for the garden even though it was chilly. I was told that I should have my shoes on. This was blamed for the cold that I caught. I became very sick. Finally I was taken to Red Cloud, Nebraska to the doctor who said that I had infected ears and it was very serious. We did not go to the regular doctor for some reason but to the new doctor who had recently opened a practice in Red Cloud. He recommended that I be taken to the larger town of Hastings, Nebraska where a Doctor could perform a new type of operation at the Mary Lanning Hospital. He would call and set up the procedure for six the next morning. We went home and got up the next morning at four am only to find out that we had a flat tire. Dad jacked up the car and patched the inner tube before we could start. Would we make it on time? It was ten miles to Red Cloud and another 50 miles on to Hastings over gravel roads that were rough and dusty. As we walked into the hospital entrance a large grandfather clock was striking six. I have been told this is what happened. I have very dim memories. I was six years old.

When I was being prepped I remember being asked if I could count and I proudly started but only got to five or six as the ether was applied to put me to sleep. I remember waking in a large room in a high bed all alone. I slid down to the floor and felt dizzy. The floor was cold and I went to the door and started down the hall. Evidently a nurse saw me and hustled me back to bed. The operation consisted of chiseling the bone behind both ears to reach the mastoid cavities and drain and clean them of the infection. My head was wrapped around and around to protect the wounds. I know it was difficult to sleep as it was painful to lie on my back and side so I laid face down which made it hard to breathe.

I must have been in the hospital for an extended time, but I don't remember. When I did go home I had to be brought back regularly to change the bandages. I remember stopping in Red Cloud at Sid's Café to get a ten cent hamburger and an orange drink on the way. I did not like carbonated beverages so always had pop without any fizz. When we started going once a week or so I can remember it being hot so it must have been later in the summer. I remember them calling it "irrigating my ears." After the bandage was unwound, water would be run over the wounds to clean them before rewrapping the bandages. It must have been difficult for dad as he had to drive because mother never learned. He had do the farming and then drive the sixty miles up and then back from Hastings. It seems that he was with me during the operation. The doctor wanted to take out my tonsils and adenoids, but dad said that I had had enough. I don't remember mother being at the hospital. She stayed for a time nearby in a house. They never complained about anything.

Dad was upset when I came down with the German measles. I must have been exposed at the hospital. I remember having to stay in bed with the blinds drawn so the lights wouldn't harm my eyes. It was hot. I remember mother placing her wrist watch close to my ears and then slowly moving it farther away to check if I could hear normally. The hospital receipt was dated 1937 for $32.60 and marked paid.

On one of the last trips to the hospital, as they were cleansing my ears, a small coca cola glass filled with crushed ice and root beer (I think) had evidently been placed there as a treat. I had never had a carbonated drink so I wouldn't drink it.

The operation was quite an ordeal to go through. Somewhat later they started just drilling a hole into the mastoid cavity to drain the infection as I have heard. Of course with penicillin and other drugs, the operation is no longer needed. Small tubes as placed in the ear drum to relieve pressure. My daughter had this done when she had her tonsils removed. She has a slight hearing loss due to not knowing fluid was being trapped in the mastoid cavity. We thought it was cute as a small child she pronounced basement as just base. She wasn't hearing the last syllable and we felt bad that we had not had it corrected sooner.

This whole affair had a huge impact on my life. My ears remained very sensitive for a long time. I would not participate in contact sports such as wrestling, boxing or football. I avoided rough-housing with other boys and kept them at arms length. This was a problem in high school.

$ 32 60

MARY LANNING MEMORIAL HOSPITAL 4/29/37

each

Hastings, Nebr.

RECEIVED OF C. A. Stones for Norman Stones

	DOLLARS
For Room Charges 4/24 - 4/29	12 50
For Anaesthetic	7 50
For Operating ~~and Delivery~~ Room	7 50
For Special Nurse's Board	
For Dressings and Sutures	1 30
For X-Ray	
For Laboratory	1 50
For Medicine	50
For Laundry	30
For Assistant Fee	
For Miscellaneous Matthiesen Drug Co	1 50
	32.60

Mary Lanning Memorial Hospital

(By) _____

Hospital No. XI

Rock Road

One warm day when I was about 5 years old I heard a loud noise coming from the road. The sound got louder and louder. It was a rock crusher being pulled along and dumping the crushed rock on the roadway. Men with shovels walked behind and made sure the rock was evenly distributed. They shouted out when they say me. I remember being told to stay back. This was a WPA (Works Project Administration) job to make the road surface "all weather." It worked quite well for many years until the rock sunk into the mud or was pushed into the grader ditches. While the bottom of my feet were calloused from going barefoot in warm weather, the sharp edges on the rocks made walking on it uncomfortable. Gravel must have been too expensive. It is still called the rock road to this day but it is mostly dirt.

My mother used to tell the story of when I was just a little tyke. I would pull my little red wagon over the yard and come up to the kitchen door and yell "mommy" and she would stop whatever she was doing and I would say, "I got some kindling for you". She would take the sticks and corn cobs and let me know that was a help. Many times when she had to walk to the back of the pasture to round up the cattle and bring them in to be milked, she would pull me in the red wagon as I would tire quickly. I also had a smaller wagon that I would tie to be back to drag along. She must have had the patience of Job as they say.

I was a helper in other ways too. I had no siblings or close cousins so I would walk around the yard and upset stumps or turn boards over. There would always be worms or bugs of some kind exposed. The chickens would rush over and gobble up anything they spotted. Some of the hens would follow me all around the yard until they were full. At night we shut the door on the chicken house to protect the chickens from predators. There were sloping boards from ceiling to floor with cross pieces for the hens to roost on. On the east side were boxes about waist high with straw in them for the hens to lay eggs. When you went to get eggs from beneath a hen sitting on the nest, you moved quickly or you would get pecked with a sharp bill. Tentative folks were afraid to gather the eggs for that reason.

Many years later I still did more "helping." Dad and I rode in the hayrack pulled by a team of horses to the field about one half mile from the barn. The cane had been cut, dried, bound into bundles and put into large shocks. We threw the bundles one by one into the hayrack to take back to the barn for feeding the livestock during the winter. There were many mice that hid under the bundles in the shock. As the bundles were moved the mice would scurry under cover. When the last bundle was picked up, the mice would run trying to find shelter. I stomped on a whole lot of them and put them in my winter coat pocket. When we got back to the barn, I went up to the house and called the cats. We usually had anywhere from 3 to a dozen hanging around. I emptied my pocket and threw the mice on the porch floor. The cats were eating the mice and trying to keep other cats away. The cats always start with the head and eat back to the tail. Since the tail is long and stringy, we said they saved the tail for a toothpick.

I had one experience that was traumatic. I must have been 5 or 6 years old. My older cousin and his two sons came by in the wagon and stopped to see if I wanted to go with them to the "80" which was a half mile west and almost a mile south. The team of horses walked along slowly and they were taking a horse to pasture there and had a rope around his neck to lead him along. I jumped at the chance and mom let me go. We had not gone far and started playing with the rope by winding it around our hands and quickly unwinding it. While it was wrapped around my hands, the horse was startled and stopped and jerked his head up. This jerked me the length of the wagon. My new coat that had just come in the mail caught on a nail and tore it almost half in two beyond repair. My teeth had cut the inside of lower lip that caused me to bleed a lot. One small flap never did heal over and is a reminder to this day. I was taken back home and mom did not place any blame but indicated that I should have been more careful.

An Annual View.

Spring is a wonderful time of year. The snows are usually over and the weather is starting to warm. The cows have had their baby calves in February. It is time to prepare the fields for planting the crops. Dad, one time wanted to farm a small field that had not been cultivated before. It was necessary to first plow the soil. He used a one-bottom plow to turn the soil over. He had coated the plow with axle grease to prevent it from rusting. After plowing for a short time the plow was as shiny as chrome. One team of horses could pull the plow as he walked behind it holding on to the handles to guide it and control how deep the blade went. He let me try but I was too small to control the depth and direction with the horses reins around my neck. The next step was to disc the ground. Four horses were hooked to the disc that had a series of circular blades that cut through the soil and smoothed it. There was a seat to sit on as the horses drug the disc along. Heavy rocks were put on the disc to get it to go deeper into the soil. To make the soil finer sometimes a rectangular framework with teeth pointing down, called a harrow, was drug over the ground to break up any clods. Today with "no till" farming all of this work is not necessary.

Of course the vegetable garden was prepared for planting. Seed potatoes were cut into pieces so that one potato could make many plants if an eye were left on the piece. I remember trying to help as a little boy and was told about the eyes. We would plant 20 long rows or more around Good Friday. In a few months mom would take a large fork and dig under the plant and harvest small potatoes that she would cream or cut in half and fry. New fresh vegetables were very tasty after eating the old potatoes from the year before. Fried potatoes and home-made bread and milk with onion was a frequent supper. In the fall dad would plow up the rows of potatoes and we would pick up many sacks full and take them to the cellar under the house and pile them against the dirt wall on the dirt floor and put up boards to hold them in a big pile. They would last until the next spring but would need to be sprouted every so often to keep them firm and keep them from rotting. That was usually my job as I got older. Sometimes a snake got into the cellar so I was usually watchful. The only light came from the open door unless you took a kerosene lantern with you. There were shelves down there where mom stored the peaches, blue plums, tomato juice and meat that she had canned. Other vegetables planted were both round red and long icicle whites radishes, onions, peas, green beans, lettuce, tomatoes and squash. Some years we would plant several long rows of sweet corn. We had field corn in other fields for selling. Sometimes we ate that too as roasting ears. It was not as sweet but tasted okay if picked early.

With the soil prepared, it was time to plant the corn. The lister machine had bins on top to store the seed corn. As it was pulled along, small plows dug a trench, throwing up dirt into a ridge. The seed was dropped one at a time in the bottom of the furrow. A couple of small wheels rolled over the covered seeds to pack the dirt down around the seeds. Root worms were once a major problem as they would eat the heart of the seed and nothing would grow. Later we used poisoned seed to kill the worms. If we received heavy rains, the dirt would wash down from the ridge and cover the seeds to deep to sprout. Then, replanting would be necessary. The seeds were planted in the bottom of the furrow to catch any moisture that fell. Too little rather than too much rain was usually more of a problem. When the plants had grown a foot or more, it was time to cultivate. Early in the morning the horses were rounded up and put into the barn to be fed. After our breakfast that mom had prepared, we put the harness on the horses and hooked them all together, Dad would then walk a half mile or so to the field and begin. The cultivator was pulled along and small plows threw the dirt off the ridge to support the plants. There was an old saying that the corn should be knee high by the fourth of July. The corn would "tassel" and put out a shoot at the top that would fertilize the plants. A very hot summer job for young folks was to go through the field and de-tassel the corn plants. The ears formed on the stalks and in the fall, the plants dried and turned brown. Now it was time to shuck the corn. Dad would hook a team of horses to a wagon that had a tall "bang board" on one side. As the wagon was pulled through the field, we walked along, grabbed an ear, husked it and threw it against the bang board to fall in the wagon. The horses would stop until we were too far away to hit the bang board and dad would make clicking sounds to get them to move forward. There were two kinds of devices to help remove the husks from the ears. One kind fit on the thumb and had a sharp metal end to break the husk loose from the ear. The kind I liked better fit on your hand and a strap fastened a curved metal point on your palm. You could hold an ear with one hand and pull the point into the husk to remove it. Dad usually planted white "open pollinated" corn. The ears were very long and difficult to pick and shuck. I submitted some at the county fair and won first prize. Of course, I was the only one who submitted that type of corn. Farmers were starting to use "hybrid" seed corn. It had a lot of advantages as the yields were better and it was a lot easier to shuck. One disadvantage was that sometimes you lost some ears as they would fall off on the ground before you could shuck them. Sometimes in the late fall it would snow and it was cold when you shucked. We usually had on thin white mittens. The snow would be on the corn ears so your hands would get cold from the wet snow. Of course you would wear 4 buckle overshoes as you walked through the muddy, snowy field. This was a reason to get an education and work indoors. An old saying was: Get an education as they can't take that away from you. One year we had a bumper crop. Dad made a container with some fencing in a large circle and made it 10 feet high. It was filled to the top with ears of corn. One day a truck came and loaded the corn and took it to the elevator in town. That was a pretty good income. On the farm, your income depended on selling crops or animals. You didn't have a monthly check. No rain or hail from storms meant that your income went down.

We would rotate the crops. One year or more was corn and then we would drill wheat. A difference was that we planted winter wheat that was planted in the fall. Dad would borrow a drill from one of the neighbors and after the ground was prepared, pull the drill back and forth over the field. The drill had storage bins on top to hold the seed. 10 or 12 rows were planted on each pass. As it was pulled along a small trench was cut and the seed dropped in. Wheels rolled along and covered and packed down the dirt over the seed. The seed would sprout and the field would be green. During the winter the plants would go dormant and be covered with snow. In the spring the plants would start growing and grow tall. In July we paid someone to combine the wheat and haul it to the elevator in town. Again heavy rains or hail when the wheat was ready to harvest could wipe you out or lower your yield significantly. A summer job for high school students was to go to Texas and work for someone harvesting wheat for farmers. It was long hours but good pay. As the crops ripened the crews would move north to Oklahoma, then Kansas, Nebraska and the Dakotas. A long hot job and you could get a good tan and come away with a good paycheck.

Before combines were available, we harvested the wheat differently. I was just old enough to shovel wheat from the wagon into the granary. First the wheat was cut with a binder machine. It cut the wheat and bound it into bundles, that were tied with a coarse string we called "binder twine." The two feet long bundles were then stacked into shocks with the heads up to dry. When the day arrived to thresh the wheat careful preparation was required. The Fruit family used their John Deere tractor to pull the threshing machine to our farm. The neighboring six or eight farmers arrived with their team and hayracks. When the dew had evaporated from the wheat, pitchforks were used to pitch the bundles into the hayracks and drive back to the thresher. The thresher was connected with a long belt to the John Deere flywheel. The tractor was started and the thresher began operating. A hayrack would pull up close to the thresher and the bundles or sheaves were thrown on the thresher and were shaken to knock the wheat out and down where it was collected and an auger moved the wheat into a wagon. The straw was blown out into a pile that would be ten feet high by the end of the day. When the wagon was full of wheat, another wagon was pulled up to catch the grain. My cousin, Jim and I drove the team to the granary and shoveled the wheat with a large scoop shovel through a window into the storage granary. Meanwhile the ladies had been busy preparing a big meal of fried chicken, mashed potatoes and gravy, green beans and other goodies. At noon work was stopped while the men washed and came in to enjoy the tasty meal. Tea was made with cool water from the windmill as a welcome drink. A story mom liked to tell was my Aunt Ruby had a large bowl of mashed potatoes that slipped out of her buttery hands and slid across the kitchen floor under the cabinet. She just scooped them back into the bowl and said that if any dark specks were spotted it could be pepper. After a brief time, the threshing started again until late evening when the last sheaves were brought in from the field.

Other jobs had to be completed such as hauling feed in from the field to feed the livestock during the winter. In the field one half mile south of the barn sometimes we planted cane which grew five or six feet tall. It was cut and bundled and stacked into shocks. I remember one cool sunny fall day I helped dad load the bundles of hay on the hayrack. I would lie on top of the hay that was stacked six feet or higher than the bottom of the floor of the hayrack as we hauled it back near the barn where we stacked it in large piles. It would be pitched across the fence when the cows and horse4s needed feed in the winter. It was hard work when snow was deep. I would lie on my back and watch puffy clouds in the blue sky as we jiggled and swayed through the pasture. The air would be cool, but the sun was warm on my face. As you moved the outer bundles, field mice would crawl to the middle of the shock. When the last bundle was pulled up, mice would run in all directions. I had on a heavy coat and four buckle overshoes. I would stomp on as many mice as I could and put them in my coat pocked with my gloved hand. When we got back to the house, I would call the cats. We always had a number of cats. I threw the mice onto the porch and the cats started grabbing them and eating and grabbing another so that another cat couldn't have it. I can vouch that the cat always starts eating at the head end and save the tail for a toothpick.

Another feed was alfalfa. It had to be harvested a couple of times a year. First, a team of horses pulled the mowing machine through the field that left the hay on the ground. The machine had a seven foot long sickle that had triangular blades all along it that had to be sharpened so it would cut cleanly. After several days the alfalfa was dry and a trip rake was drawn by a team of horses to make windrows. The rake was about eight feet long and had long circular teeth. After traveling a distance the teeth would be full and a lever was stepped on that raised the teeth quickly to leave a long pile of hay. After the field was all in windrows, the stacking began. A team of horses pushed a device with long wooden teeth until about a windrow was loaded. Then it was driven to where the stack was to be and dumped the hay onto another device with long wood teeth. Another team of horses pulled a rope to lift the hay and dump it on the stack. My cousin and I would use a pitchfork to move the hay about to make it level and even. On a hot day we would have our shirts off and be sweating. Sweat bees would land on us and sting our backs. The seven acre field would make a stack about ten feet high. In later years, dad would hire someone to cut and bale the alfalfa. The square bales would be loaded and moved over near the barn. My mother and sister would handle them as dad's health deteriorated in later years. He finally purchased a small Ford/Ferguson tractor after I had moved to town that made it easier than using horses. The bales were held together by two baling wires that had to be cut when the hay was fed to the animals. We purchased large blocks of salt so the animals could lick it and provide a source of sodium for their diet. The salt was just placed on a high spot of ground. Otherwise the animals would chew on fence posts and other wood around the barn. Most alfalfa is now baled in huge circular bales that need to be moved with a tractor.

It seemed as if there was always something that needed fixing. A lot of things we could do with baling wire but the well and windmill needed special tools and knowledge. We drove over to see the windmill repair man when we needed that expertise. He was an elderly bachelor who had Parkinson's disease so his hands shook. He would climb up the windmill tower and work without hanging on and without a belt or some way to secure himself, He was very frugal and would get free bones from the butcher shop and boil them with beans so he passed gas often. His saying was, "you don't want to hold those things in you, it will bust your belly." That excused it as far as he was concerned. He would show up with his flat bed truck with his tools and go to work. Our foot valve had to be replaced once which meant we had to pull the well. He had a device to keep the pipe from falling into the well as he pulled the sections of pipe up and unscrewed them and set them aside until he reached the foot valve and replaced it. I think there were about five ten foot sections. The process was reversed to lower the valve down into the well. Inside the pipe was a long steel rod that worked the valve. The rod was connected to the windmill so that when the fan blades turned by the wind, the gears made the rod go up and down. There was a small leak hole down below the frost line so that the water would not freeze and burst the pipe in the sub-zero temperatures in the winter. This small hole would rust and over time be so big that too much water fell back into the well and that section of pipe would have to be replaced. One time when I was home from the army on leave, dad asked if I would change the oil in the gear-box at the top of the tower. I climbed up the tower as steps made that possible. At the top was a platform, but it was small and you needed to lean out to do any work. I had no knowledge about how to open the box or change the oil so I climbed back down and said that we should call the repair man. I would even pay for it.

We usually had about ten milk cows. With the bull and yearlings there were about 25 cattle. After about a year or so, we would load the young animals into a truck and take them to the sale barn in town to be sold to the highest bidder .The bull would impregnate the cows as they came in heat. He could tell by putting his nose in the cow's urine stream. After several years he would impregnate his children and grand children when we kept the best animals. After too many generations, the calves would be born with unusual characteristics. We would take the bull to town and sell him so someone else could use him. We would get another young bull and turn him loose in the pasture. We were cautious until he became adjusted to his surroundings. We would have to round up the cattle wherever they were grazing and bring them to the barn to be milked morning and night. Mom did most of the milking and had a grip that was vey strong. After the cows had their calves in the spring they came fresh and started giving milk. For a time there was blood in the milk that was good for the calves as they nursed. After a time the calves were weaned and the milk was taken to the separator in the house. The milk was poured into a large bowl shaped container on top. The crank was turned to make the unit spin. After getting up to speed, a valve was opened to let the milk run down into the spinning discs. The cream was separated and ran down a pipe to a so-called gallon can. It was called so-called as it was

16

not an exact gallon but nearly a gallon. The cans were saved from buying large tin cans of fruit. The milk ran down another pipe into a bucket. This was fed to the calves to supplement the grass they ate and the small amount of milk that was left in the udder after milking. . The cream was saved into a large cream can to take to town and sold. The heavy cream tasted good on cereal and in coffee. Some would be churned into butter with a churn that was a large glass jar with a handle to turn paddles inside. In hot weather we put the churn in cool water from the windmill so the butter would form more quickly. Mom always liked the buttermilk that was the liquid left after the glob of butter was removed. The milk that was left after the cream was separated out was taken back to the barn to feed to the calves. It was necessary to teach the calves to drink from the bucket. You had to push their head down so their nose was into the milk. You put your hand down below their nose and put your middle finger in their mouth. They knew to suck so they started drinking. As they sucked, their tongue squeezed your finger and pulled on it. The tongue was rough and sliding it down helped pull the milk out of the cow's teats. We usually said tits and there were four good sized ones on the udder and two smaller ones in the back. Soon they just started drinking with no coaxing. As long as you kept milking the cows, they kept producing milk until later in the fall when they went dry. After birthing a calf in the spring they came fresh again and began to produce milk. At first there was some blood in the milk which was good for the calf, but we did not use it. Sometimes the cows ate wire grass that made the milk taste bad. When the other grass became available the milk was okay.

In addition to the cattle, dad always had several head of horses. Using four head to pull the lister and cultivator was hard work and at times the horses would be rotated. If a mare was due to have a baby colt, she could not work as long or hard and another horse would take her place. Dad would care for the horses needs. Their hoofs would have to be trimmed so they would not grow too long and split and get sore. Dad would trim the hard hooves with a sharp corn knife and a hammer. Sometimes the horses got sores on their necks from the horse collar. The skin would be rubbed raw and dad would put axle grease on the sore to keep the flies away and not get infected. All of the male horses were castrated. In order to have colts born and grow into work horses the mares had to be impregnated. One farmer had a stud horse that we used. I remember riding in the back seat of the car with my dad and uncle. I held the halter rope of the mare as we drove slowly the two or three miles to the farm where the stud horse was located. The mare was in heat and the stud could tell. He was kept in the barn and the lot was fenced with a high strong fence. The mare was led into a space with panels on both sides. The farmer brought the stud out of the barn with a strong rope. Dad told me to stay away a good distance as the horse was wild and hard to control. The stud knew what he was there for and nipped the mare on the rump and she jumped. Then the stud mounted the mare. The long, stiff, member was guided by the farmer into the mare. On the second thrust it was done. The stud was led back into the barn. We made the return trip home and in the spring we had a new baby colt.

Extremes:

Although there was some beautiful weather in the spring and fall, there were some unpleasant days in the winter and summer. The wind blew almost constantly which was tiresome. In the summer it was hot and dry and dusty. We did appreciate the wind as it turned the windmill and pumped water out of the well into the large tanks for watering the livestock. When there was a short time that it was calm, we had to manually pump the water. It would take hours of pumping to water very many animals. We would fill a bucket and carry it to the house and set it on the washstand for drinking. We kept a long handled dipper in the bucket where we drank out of the dipper when we were thirsty. That was probably not too sanitary. There was a lot of iron in the water so the bucket and dipper were stained brown.

REA (Rural Electrification Authority) meant that you could run in power from the road, but dad would not, because it meant a monthly bill and we didn't have income unless we sold something. At night we would light a kerosene lamp that would be left on until we went to bed. In the summer it would be hot in the house so we kept the windows open to catch any breeze. By morning, the heat would be gone and it would be so cool that you needed to cover up.

In the winter, temperatures would be below freezing some days. A fire was kept going in the kitchen cook stove all day and the rest of the house was cold. We had an oil burner stove in the living room but seldom used it. At one time it was a wood burning stove but updated to the kerosene heater. Oil was kept in a 55, gallon drum outside and fuel was transferred from that into a spouted container and then into a tank on the stove. We let the fire die down in the kitchen and go to bed in the unheated bedrooms. We wore flannel pajamas. Sometimes, mom would wrap one of her irons that was kept on the stove in a towel and put it at the foot of the bed as the floor and bedclothes were freezing. It felt good to put your feet down and find a warm spot. Mom used the heavy irons to iron the clothes. Monday was wash day and water was heated and put in the wash tub. The clothes were then rubbed on a wash-board in the hot water with homemade lye soap to get them clean. Another tub was full of rinse water and the clothes wrung by hand to remove most of the water. The clothes would be taken out to the clothes line and hung up with clothes pins. In the cold weather, the clothes would freeze dry and be stiff when taken down. Later we purchased a powered washing machine that had a small gasoline motor to turn the agitator and wringer. The motor had a kick starter and was often hard to start as it was hard to keep tuned. One day after the clothes were all up, the pole broke that held the line up and the clothes fell on the muddy ground. That meant that the clothes had to be re-washed and rehung to dry. That was the fastest I ever saw dad fix something as mom was not a happy camper. Tuesday mom ironed the clothes. The irons had an opening to attach a wood handle. She would sprinkle water on the clothes to make them damp and then take an iron from the stove when it was hot and iron the wrinkles out. The irons would cool quickly so she would put the iron back on the stove, remove the handle and attach another iron. She tested the iron by spitting on her finger and touching the iron to see hot it was. She kept rotating the irons until everything was done.

The fire would die out in the kitchen stove so it got cold enough that the water in the bucket would freeze by morning. Mom would be the first one up and would shake the ashes down through the grates into the ash drawer that had to be emptied regularly. Then with newspaper, sticks, corn cobs and a little kerosene start a fire to warm the kitchen. As the fire grew larger pieces of wood or coal would be added to make a lot of heat. Sometimes the top of the stove would get red hot. After the stove was hot, I would get up and stand on the oven door to get warm. The floor was ice cold. When I was small, I fell over on the stove and was burned. For a long time my sore side was an excuse to get my way.

Flies

Most of the animals went to the bathroom whenever they felt the need. Flies laid their eggs in the feces and when the weather was hot in the summer flies were around by the thousands. The cows and horses would switch their tails to scare the flies away, but many were able to bite the animals. There were also some large horse flies too, but the smaller ones were the most prevalent. One time we mixed powdered DDT with water and sprayed it on the backs of the cattle to help protect them. Many flies would sit on the screen door to the kitchen and would fly inside when you went in or out. Sometimes we used fly-paper that was sticky and attracted the flies. They would land on the paper and be stuck. Sometimes mom would get out the sprayer and spray all inside the kitchen. We would put a tea towel over the water pail when we would go to town. By the time we returned, most of the flies had been killed. The towel prevented the flies from falling into the drinking water. At night we would light the kerosene lamp and the screen door would be covered with flies that were attracted to the light. I have seen dad take a few pages of newspaper and make a torch that he would sweep up and down the door on the outside. The flies would be killed or their wings burned so that they could not fly. It didn't help much because there would soon be hundreds more, but psychologically one might feel better.

Grasshoppers

When the weather warmed, grasshopper eggs would hatch from where they had been buried in the ground and when you walked through the grass, they would fly in all directions. There were many varieties. Some were small, others grew large and some were quite fat. The larger ones made good bait for fishing. You would hold the hopper and put a hook into his head and down through his body. When captured, the hopper would emit a brown liquid that we called tobacco juice. I suppose the brown liquid would protect it from other predators. Some years they were worse but none as bad as during the dust bowl when they ate everything green and even the fence posts. Another sight was stink bugs. They got into the fresh cow dung and make a ball like a fairly large marble. Two insects would work together rolling the ball along. I think they laid their eggs in the ball and left it to hatch more bugs. The cow dung would dry in the hot sun so that you ended up with a disk a foot or more in diameter and a couple of inches thick. We never used the cow chips, but they made pretty good fuel for burning in the stove as the trees had all died in the drought years of the dust bowl so there was not much wood available. In the fall most small towns had a celebration put on by the business bureau. Lebanon, Kansas had the Lebanon Anniversary. A carnival came to town and excitement was in the air. We rode the merry-go-round and Ferris wheel and other rides. I was afraid of heights so when I rode the Ferris wheel with my cousin, we would stop on top and he would rock the seat. I was really glad when that ride ended.

Tough tasks

Many of the tasks to be done were not always a lot of fun. I remember one time when I helped dad castrate the young pigs. I would help hold them down and dad used his knife that had been sharpened carefully. He would squeeze the sac until it was tight and then make a cut of a couple inches and the testicle would slide out. He would pull and a long tube would come out. He would pour some disinfectant on the wounds and let them go. By doing this, the pigs would grow large for meat and their desire to fight other males would be gone. It was cheaper to do it yourself than to hire someone if you could find someone.

I remember helping butcher a pig. It was done when the weather was getting cold so the meat would not spoil as we had no refrigeration. Early in the morning, a large oval boiler would be filled with water and heated to boiling. An empty 55 gallon drum was set up under the front porch. Corn was put in the trough to attract the pigs. One was selected and my dad would shoot it between the eyes with our 22 caliber rifle. My Uncle Floyd would quickly slit its throat with a large butcher knife to bleed all the blood out. By this time, hot water had been put in the barrel. The pig was dragged down to the porch and with the use of a block and tackle raised up and put into the hot water in the barrel. Ashes from the cook stove were used in the water. After raising and lowering the pig in the water several times, it was laid out on a low table. Then, using sharp knives the entire pig would be shaved to remove all the hair. When finished, the skin was white and smooth. Dad, my uncle and older cousin took turns. Then it was time to pull the pig into the air and cut it's stomach open to remove the intestines (offal). The head was cut off and the liver cleaned up to fry right away. That was the first meal and all were hungry by afternoon. I did not like liver so they would cut some side meat and fry it. It was like bacon but not cured. The carcass was cut up and the hams and shoulders were salted and put in a large crock to keep. Mom would take the tenderloin and save it for breakfast meals. It was very lean and tasty with biscuits. She saved all the scraps and made a large bowl of sausage. She used sage seasoning and I still enjoy the taste. Meat from the head was cooked and put in a cloth and twisted to remove the fat. This was hung up and after a few days could be sliced as lunch meat. We called it head cheese. Since the tenderloin was taken out, there were no pork chops. The side meat sometimes was smoked in a low building. It was my job to keep a small fire smoking and filling the building. It made tasty bacon.

Once in the spring, a cow was in trouble trying to birth a calf. Dad and I went and assessed the situation. She was lying down in the barn. He decided that the calf was trying to come out head first but had it twisted back and was too large for the opening. He was able to put his arm into the birth canal and push it back and get the head in the proper location. The calf was born and all was well. She delivered a short time later. To lose a calf and a cow would have been a big loss.

I only remember butchering a beef one time. Again it was in very cold weather. The animal was killed by hitting it on top of the head with an ax. In this case, the calf was skinned and cut up. It was not bled as with pork and the result was red meat. The carcass was hung up in the granary that was empty and would freeze during cold weather. Mom would go out and with a butcher knife and cut off steak to take in and fry. Some would be run through a meat grinder to make hamburger. The grinder was screwed onto the kitchen counter and had a handle to turn and move the meat through small holes. Different plates could be used with different size holes. Some meat was cooked and canned to have later as with the small family, we could not always eat the whole beef.

Of course there were coyotes to contend with, skunks and other varmints such as jack rabbits and cotton tail rabbits. There were quail and pheasants, but I don't remember any wild turkeys. My cousin trapped skunks in the winter and sold the skins to make some money.

Grade School

I turned 5 on March 17, 1938 (Saint Patrick's Day) and started to school in September in the first grade. There was no kindergarten then. This had an impact on my life as I graduated high school at 17. My mother walked with me for a time until I was brave enough to walk by myself and join my two older cousins, Charles and Harold on the way. It was ½ mile east and ½ mile north of the farm house. We walked in mud and snow and were lucky when the road was dry. As you turned into the driveway for the school grounds from the road there was a pump where we could pump water to put in the container inside the school building. Each student had a tin cup hanging on a nail to use for drinking. There was a "merry-go-round" in front of the one room school.

North of the school was a small building for storage of fuel for the stove. I remember there were remains of an organ where we removed the brass reeds that made the sounds. Between the school and this building was a below ground cellar. It was concrete with steps down to go in case of a storm like a tornado or cyclone. On the northwest corner of the school grounds was the girl's outhouse and on the southwest corner was the boy's outhouse.

There were steps going in to the front of the school. There were rows of desks going south to north, small desks for the first grade, larger ones and finally larger ones for some of the big farm kids. There was a large stove where wood and coal were burned during cold weather. At the front was the teacher's desk. Dwight Corbett and I were the only first graders. Dale Ward was my teacher for the first 3 years and I give him credit for helping me study hard and do well in school. He had a cock eye which made it hard to know where he was looking. He would walk up and down the aisle as we were to be studying and make sure no one was goofing off. He would take hold of the short hair on the back of the neck and raise those who were slouching down in their seats to sit up straight. You might get your knuckles cracked with his ruler if you were caught doing what you should not be doing. I tried to make sure I didn't suffer any of those lessons.

Class by class he would have students go up front and would quiz them about their lesson. Often you could learn information from classes ahead of yours. There were large slate boards on the north wall. Sometimes at the end of the day we could go up to the board and practice writing or solving problems. You had to be careful to not use too much chalk. Taking erasers outside and pounding them together to get rid of the chalk dust was a chore that was looked forward to. You didn't have to study and you got to get out of the classroom. You really needed a bathroom before the teacher would Okay that trip.

One time late in the day another First grader and I were at the board writing. I looked and there was a puddle that he was standing in and it kept getting bigger and bigger. I knew that meant terrible consequences. As it turned out, class was dismissed and he had to stay and man the mop and nothing was ever said. From then on we made sure to not be bashful about holding up one or two fingers to let him know that we needed to go. The pencil sharpener had been mounted on the window sill but the base had broken. So the teacher would hold the device by hand and let you turn the handle to put a point on your pencil. He made sure you didn't grind too much of the pencil away.

We always had a Christmas tree and would work making decorations such as strings of pop-corn and cranberries months before. We never had a Christmas tree at home so it was a joy. The teacher would get presents to give to each student. One year he gave out ever-sharp pencils. Mine was a different color from the rest and I worried that I was being singled out or almost left out but was afraid to ask.

We played different games during recess. Some where kids would stand in a circle and some-one would run around and then tag someone and take their place. I enjoyed playing softball. The teacher would hit the ball and you would field it. I bent over to get a pretty hard grounder and it bounced and hit me in the nose. From then on I never wanted to play infield. I could catch flies and throw but I never got over the fear of ground balls. The game that I most en-joyed was Andy over. Someone would throw a rubber ball over the schoolhouse. There was a team on each side. You could catch the ball, then run around and tag one of the other team and then they would be on your side. I loved the running and excitement. We did compete with other schools in softball one year I remember. I pitched and had learned to put backspin on the ball. It was supposed to cause pop ups so we could catch the ball in the air and not have to throw ground balls to first base.

We put on plays at special times like Christmas and performed them for the parents who had come for the PTA meeting. Wires were strung from wall to wall and curtains of sheets made a good stage. My teachers the last 5 years of school were all female. When I was in the 8th grade, the next oldest student was my cousin, who was in the 5th grade. When I graduated from the 8th grade we went to the county seat of Smith Center, Kansas. We walked across the stage and received our diploma. My mother bought me a vested suit, new shoes and a dress hat. She took my picture with her box camera and had a 5X8 picture made and framed it. She had taken the 8th grade twice but never went to high school and my father did not either.

I remember some of the families. One had several children and lived somewhere north of the school. One was older and would challenge the boxer when the carnival came to town. I think one boy was in the 8th grade when I started school and was slim and rangy. His brother was heavyset and seemed effeminate we would say now. Their sister was near my age and could have benefited from deodorant as I remember. One girl was a little younger than me I think, but I thought she was cute. She lived one mile east and a little south of the school.

One other family that I remember lived one mile east of the school. The father had an oversized middle finger on his right hand I think it was. The mother was a good wife. Their oldest was a son, then another son, another son a daughter and then twin girls. One was about my age and heavy set. I was s skinny beanpole. Somehow, the kids were urging me to confront him for something that I do not remember. I wanted no part in any kind of activity like that but we ended up pushing or shoving and I think he pushed me down. That ended the affair. Perhaps the teacher came out. When we were in our 70s, he and I met at a funeral and had not seen each other since grade school. I mentioned something about the episode and he remembered how I had wrongly done things. He still felt that I had been the culprit, but I think I was too much of a coward to have done it alone. A mob of kids pushing is my thinking. Bullying happens everywhere.

Another family had a daughter who was a tall slender girl who was not very good scholastically. She was made fun of as I remember and I felt sorry for her. They lived about a mile west of the school. Another daughter was about my age and went on to be successful.

Spare time

During the summer with no siblings or nearby friends and my parents working the farm, I often needed something to do. When I was very young, I would run away and go down the road where my cousins lived. They had a dog who would follow you and nip your heel when you ran. That hurt. At one time they had a Billy goat that would come up behind you when you were not looking and butt you. But there were lots of good times with them. I had a girl cousin who was younger and she would come down to play. Mother would have to walk over to get me and usually brought a switch. My mother took me to the library in town to get me involved in reading. I read the whole series of books named "The Bobbsey Twins". There were a dozen books or so. I also made toys. I would break a long corn cob in half. The core is a soft white material. I would insert two chicken feathers into the core and then when you threw it up in the air it would spin like a helicopter as it fell. The lid of a coffee can was sharp so I would pound the rim down and throw it like a Frisbee. I obtained a hard cover red book that told how to make all sorts of things. I made sling shots that we called nigger shooters. I learned later that was not a polite term to use. Rubber cut from an old inner tube was used with a Y shaped tree branch and leather to make the seat for the pebble or rock. The rubber was often old and would snap if you tried to pull too hard. A cousin lived with us for a while and he showed how to make and fly kites which I enjoyed. I made a whistle out of a slippery elm tree branch and whittled some with my knife. I liked to make tops to spin out of wood thread spools. I made a place to jump and would raise and lower the bar. I whittled a two by four down to use as a vaulting pole. One time I was up in the air when the two by four broke. There had been a nail hole near the middle and it was weak. I would get orange crates from the grocery store in town and remove the nails and had wood I could use to make things. Using a coping saw I would make what-not shelves which we could hang on the wall to put small items. I used the nails that I took out of the orange crate as I took it apart. I made a small table which we still had years later.

By far, the thing that helped me most in later years was the time I spent practicing pitching. A few box tops from Wheaties cereal boxes and a few cents mailed to the company would get me a little book about baseball pitchers. I remember Bob Feller and his 100 miles per hour fast ball from Iowa. Another pitcher threw side arm or under handed so I practiced for hours. I had a rubber ball about the size of a regular baseball. In grade school we used a soft ball. I would scratch a rectangle on the side of the barn to represent the strike zone. I would throw against the barn and practice fielding the ball is it came back on the ground. I got to where I could hit the corners or right down the middle. I lacked speed but had excellent control after hours and hours of pitching. I made sure to wind up and follow through correctly. This was the thing that showed me how important it was to practice and be persistent. When Junior Legion baseball was started the summer after my freshman year, my practice paid off.

High School

My grandfather and grandmother were living on the homestead with my father and his older brother. Families would gather on Sunday to share meals and play games. My grandfather was known as the fastest runner in Smith County. My older cousin once told me that he had seen him strap heavy weights to his feet to build up the muscles in his legs as he walked and farmed the fields. At some point he was ill and evidently went to the Mayo clinic. I had seen receipts in an old desk when I was a child. Evidently he had asthma and he moved to Akron, Colorado for the climate. My grandmother on my mother's side had done the same thing. One fall when the crops had been harvested, my dad bought a new 1930 Chevrolet and drove out to visit. He met my mother there and they were married in two weeks. They came back to Kansas and moved into the house with my uncle and his wife. Some time after that, Zell and my grandmother moved back. The house was too small for 3 families, so my uncle moved to another farm to be a sharecropper. Some time later, my grandfather moved to Red Cloud, Nebraska to work in a creamery. He and my grandmother purchased a house. So dad stayed and farmed and gave a portion of the income to his father. My grandfather wanted to run some cattle in addition which meant dad would not be able to have a larger herd. Somehow it worked out.

The year I was to start high school a bus from Lebanon, Kansas was not run to pick up children in our area. Whether it was because of funding or not having a driver I do not know. Driving down and dropping me off and going back in the afternoon was not feasible and I was too young at 13 to drive myself. The solution was that I would move in with my grandmother. My grandfather had died some time prior so she agreed. I don't know how much she charged for my room and board. I was the only one of my relatives to go to a Nebraska school. The state of Kansas had to pay for me to go to another state. All the rest of the Stones children went to high school in Lebanon including my sister who was born in 1947.

Grandmother's house was a small, two-bed room structure with a step down kitchen. The outhouse was back at the alley. It was a nicely constructed building made as a WPA project. It had a concrete base, stool with a lid that had a spring to keep it open or closed and wood venting to move the fumes outside. It was to decided to build an indoor bathroom hooked up to the city sewer system. My dad, uncle, his son and I dug the ditch to the alley. This probably saved some money. The ditch started shallow but was deep at the alley. Once the project was complete, there was no need for the outhouse there. My dad became the owner. We planned to move it to the farm. The outhouse on the farm was attached to the chicken house just west of the house. It was decided to put the new outhouse a little further west. My job was to dig the hole to set the outhouse on. I dug and dug down to about six feet. It was hard to throw

the dirt out as I dug. One day the truck arrived and the building was set down over the hole. It served us well for many years. The indoor plumbing was very nice for us especially in cold or rainy weather. Grandmother was very saving on the water and only flushed the stool about once a day.

I was very homesick the first semester until I was used to being away from home. I had made friends and was doing well in school. My folks would come to town on Saturday evening to sell the eggs and cream and shop for groceries. Dad liked to visit the pool hall to shoot pool and drink beer. There were two pool halls in town, the north pool hall and the south pool hall. In later years he didn't bother with pool. The north pool hall had a billiard table and was felt to be a little higher class. There were also snooker tables and regular pool tables. They say a good pool shooter is the sign of a wasted youth, but it was entertaining. I would ride home with them and stay until Sunday evening when dad would drive me back in. I had found that the J. C. Penney store was looking for a janitor. I knew that money was tight as always so I wanted to earn and help out. One Sunday night as we drove down Main Street I saw a light in the Penney's store. I asked dad to stop so I could check and he said that no one would be there. He stopped and I ran to the door and looked in. Away in the back in the mezzanine I saw someone. I knocked on the door with no result. On the third knock the man got up and came to the door and asked what I wanted. When I told him he just said "come back tomorrow." I don't know if I impressed him or not but when I went back the next day he hired me. I started at 30 cents and hour and worked there 3 years and got up to 33 cents an hour. I am sure that he knew I was green and would have to be shown everything. He took me in the men's restroom and asked me if I knew what immaculate meant. Of course I had no idea. He cleaned the sink and stool and said that was immaculate and I was to keep it that way. Years later I would go back and check and it was never immaculate. I owe him a lot for letting me work there before and after school.

Since I had come from the farm, I was enrolled in a class named "Vocational Agriculture." I liked it as we got to be in the shop working with metal, wood and made rope. The first test was failed by everyone I think. Although I was usually meek, I argued about the test being unfair and thought I had some good points. After I finished, the teacher said "that test was pretty rocky wasn't it Rocky?" From then on I was known as Rocky. I had never had a nickname before as Norman did not lend itself to nicknames, but some do like just plain Norm. A good friend had broken his arm and had it in a cast. He was called "stiff arm" and another student answered the question in chemistry class of what comes out of a volcano as "hot rock" and from then on that was what he was called.

In one class we had to get up in the front of the group and talk for 3 minutes about ourselves. That was when I new what stage fright meant. I decided to take a speech course in college because of that experience.

Since I worked before and after school I was not able to go out for the usual sports, but I participated in chorus since I liked to sing. I remember one time we traveled to Kearney, Nebraska to the college there to compete with other schools. We stayed overnight in a hotel. I don't know if much sleeping got done but we sang about watching the sun go down on Galway bay the next day. I had good grades so I was sent up to Kearney to compete in mathematics tests with other students. Before I went I was allowed to go to an empty room by myself to study for the test. I think I was about 34th or 37th of 300 or more participants so I did pretty well.

My senior year the high school decided to start a baseball program. Since I had a reputation as a good pitcher from my summer evening games I pitched one game and never practiced with the team since I worked before and after school. From that I received a major letter for my sweater. Many who had played year after year in football or other sports only received the small minor letter. I felt guilty about it as it didn't seem fair but I was pleased. I do not remember ever getting the sweater to put the letter on.

One morning as I was sweeping the sidewalk in front of the J. C. Penney store, my good friend rode up on his bike. I told him I didn't feel good so he suggested we go down the street to the doctor's office. The doctor was in and asked me to open my shirt. He said that I had chicken pox. I was afraid it was smallpox but he assured me I would do Okay. I had welts all over my body and itched everywhere. I stayed in my room until the itching stopped. The staff at Penney's sent a fruit basket. I exposed the cast for a class play we were practicing, but the performance went on. One line in the play I still remember another friend said. It was "the scent emanating from your direction is not reminiscent of calla lilies."

One teacher was a strict old maid teacher. She taught math and Latin. I never took Latin but it probably would have helped me. I remember one time when she was up front during our study hall time. One boy was the son of a local man who ran the tavern. He didn't study but just sat there. She shook her finger at him and he took a book out and laid it on his desk. She shook her finger again and he opened it but didn't look down at it. Most if not all of the students were observing this. He had a full head of hair that was like a bowl cut. She walked back to his desk and grabbed a big handful of hair with one hand and slapped him hard across the face 4 times. Whap. Then she went back to the front of the room and didn't shake her finger anymore and he didn't pretend to study either. His face was very red from the slaps and maybe some embarrassment. I guess it was a draw. Now she probably would be fired or sent to jail, but we didn't mess with her. I could never get an A in her math class, but I was glad I did not have to take Latin that she taught. Now I think the Latin would have helped me.

I liked to go to the football and basketball games. I sat in the bleachers and cheered the players on with the girls. Once they asked me to help with the yard marker at one football game. I had no idea what I was doing so they finally got someone else. I was glad I didn't have to practice all the time and have to shower with all the guys. It was too embarrassing.

Overall I did pretty well in school. One time I was chosen to represent Webster County at Boy's State. I went to Lincoln and stayed with the other boys and studied how government worked. I had to have a small pox vaccination and it didn't take the first time, so I had it again later. When I was there it was scabbed over and full of puss so I couldn't go swimming. That was fine with me as I was bashful. One time a man came and showed us how to hit golf balls. I was impressed how far they flew There was a talent show at the end with different groups that been organized as different political entities performing. One group dressed as girls and acted silly that stole the show.

Phonograph

My grandmother died December 24,1947. Since I had been living with her, I had to move. I started rooming with my buddy in a small house a few blocks away where his mother and aunt lived. One warm night he and I were running around and came upon an auction sale where household goods were being sold. We saw this old phonograph and it looked nice. His mother happened to be there and we asked her to bid on it. She got it for four dollars. Somehow we got it moved to her small house.

The nameplate had this information on it: Edison Disc Phonograph model C250 serial number SM-66777 Orange New Jersey. It was about 2 feet square and just over 4 feet tall. At the top was a lid that could be propped open. On the side was the crank for winding up the springs. There was a double set of springs so you had to wind for a long time to get it fully wound. Single springs many times broke from too much winding trying to get it to play a longer time. An exponential horn curved down and sound came out a grill on the front. A lever up top moved a large soft sphere into or out of the horn to control the sound. Below were two large drawers that held the records.

After a short time, my friend's mother said it was taking up too much room and wanted to get rid of it. I was able to pay 2 or 4 dollars to her for his portion and have it moved to the farm. Since there was no electricity there, you could wind it up and have music. There were about 25 thick heavy plastic records that had recordings on both sides. Favorites were songs like Barney Google with his Goo, Goo, Googily eyes and Yes! We have no bananas. It had a diamond stylus or needle that never needed replacement. The sound was good, but there was a scratching sound where the head touched as the record turned. Once I put a microphone into the front of the horn and the recorded sound was good.

For many years it stayed on the farm where our children liked to listen to it. Finally when we had a place of our own, we moved it to Lincoln, Nebraska. Then we went to Pittsburgh, PA, then to St Louis, MO, Fort Worth, TX, then to Papillion, NE next to Guam, Mariana Islands and back to Norfolk, VA, and on to St. Mary's, GA and back to Virginia Beach, VA. It is now back with our son in Crete, NE and still works. You can adjust the speed so the sound drawls or speed it up to the best sound or very fast which the young ones liked. It also shuts off automatically when the record is finished playing. The finish is pretty worn, but it was made to last. When we moved to Guam, the movers inventoried it as an antique stereo.

After my Uncles wife died, he moved to Oregon with his two daughters to work in the wood industry. He had lived on a farm a mile away and stored his belonging in our basement. He had a newer phonograph with thinner records and was similar to the Edison except it used steel needles. The spring was single and had broken from being wound too tightly. I would turn it with my finger and listen to "When its spring time in the Rockies, I'll be coming back to you."

Guitar

I have always liked music. I asked for a banjo one Christmas when I was 7 years old. Santa always came and left the presents in the kitchen. We slept in cold bedrooms and in December it would be freezing cold. Mom would build a fire in the cook stove so the kitchen was warm when I got out of bed. That was the best Christmas ever. There sat a new large red wagon with a guitar in it. I also got a big whittling knife. The guitar had been ordered from the Montgomery Ward catalog. It was not a full size guitar. It had 1941 stamped inside of it. No one around knew anything about guitars so I read and tried to get it tuned. I finally could pick out songs one note at a time for songs I knew the tune to. I liked Gene Autry and wanted to learn chords and play the way he did. I did not know how to strum and pick in ¾ or 4/4 time. I had nothing to give me the correct pitch. I would tune the low string and the book showed how to tune the other strings from that. Sometimes I would start a little high and would snap the high e string. I would pay the jeweler 10 cents in town for a new one. You didn't need to buy a whole set of strings as now.

I remember one time when my Uncle and his wife and my cousins, visited from Ord, Nebraska. My two boy cousins were about my age and had taken piano and accordion lessons. I think my dad asked me to play something. I tried to pick out "The Atchison, Topeka and The Santa FE" song that was popular at the time. I am not sure that anyone was impressed. Ha. An older cousin's wife, played guitar and tried to show me some, but I had very little musical knowledge. There was a store in Smith Center, Kansas our county seat that sold guitars and I asked how to pick and strum. He just said that there were many ways to go about it.

My best buddy's family moved to a house a little over a mile from us. They had my buddy and 2 younger girls. He was a year younger than me. His mother played the piano and his uncle played string instruments. My buddy had a regular size "F" hole guitar. I learned how to pick and play chords. He showed me a lot so I could play along with him. We would sing duets. The one-room schools were always looking for programs for their PTA meetings. We performed several times in the evenings. I was fine with someone with me. One time I was asked to come and sing for a PTA meeting in the little town of Ionia, Kansas. My buddy could not attend for some reason. My dad drove me to the school. Wow, it was a large brick building and had a stage. It came time for me to sing and I was nervous. I played and sang "The Yellow Rose of Texas" and things went well and I sang all the verses. During the last chorus I blocked on the last line and stopped. I started the chorus over and got to that last line and again could not bring it to mind. The audience had grown very silent. Finally I started the chorus again and was able to complete the song. The audience had been quiet until then and I received a standing ovation. I was happy to be finished and did not want to perform alone again.

Once we entered a talent contest in Red Cloud, NE during Fall Festival days. We sang the song "Simple Melody". My buddy sang one part and I sang a separate part. Then we sang them at the same time. We won the contest and the music was recorded on a wire recorder and played over the radio station in the larger town of Hastings, NE although I was never able to tune in the station or listen to the song.

Someone broke into the ice plant office and took some money as we heard. It was decided that it would be a good idea to keep boys busy. A quartet was formed with a bass, baritone, second tenor and me as first tenor. We all enjoyed getting together. One mother would play the piano and help us with our parts. We were asked to sing at various events such as the father and son dinner at the Methodist church. One time a box elder bug flew in my ear while we were singing. I was slapping my ear and we all got to laughing and could hardly finish the song.

I also sang in the high school chorus. They always needed tenors so I would get to sing. One time we traveled to McCook, NE to compete with other schools. We had to stay overnight in a hotel there. I don't think we got much rest. We sang "Galway Bay", an Irish song. We didn't score too high but had fun. One buddy ended up marrying our music teacher. They moved to Lincoln, NE, and he received a degree in Architectural Engineering. They had 9 children. He and I would go in the evening to have special instruction from our music teacher. He learned more than I did.

My best buddy and I were always clowning around. I roomed with them for a short time. We had a float in a parade for Fall Festival one year to have a store name before the crowd. He drove the 1934 four, door sedan and I sat on top dressed in a ladies long dress with a sun bonnet and rocked in a rocking chair. I was lucky I didn't get thrown off and injured. I'm sure we didn't win any prize for our float. The cloth top of the car was probably never the same.

An amusing event (at least to me) was when my buddy and I were walking down town on the sidewalk and came upon another buddy. My closer buddy had a long rubber band and he went up to our other buddy and put his left hand between his eyes on his forehead and with his right hand pulled the rubber band back two or three feet and said, "stick them up". The rubber band broke and whopped our friend. He had on big heavy boots and instantly started trying to kick my buddy in the shins. He was dancing around trying to avoid the kicks and holding up the two pieces of rubber band saying, "I didn't mean to" it broke. Soon everyone calmed down and lived happily ever after.

Baseball

During the summer after high school, I stayed in town and worked rather than go help on the farm. After my freshman year our coach started a Junior Legion baseball team and I tried out. He had returned from the service and had a radio repair shop. There were just enough boys to make the 9 for a team. We practiced and played with other towns. One boy was a good athlete and could throw fast balls, but his control was not good and he would walk a lot of runs in. From my many hours of practice on the farm, I could throws strikes easily and not walk many so I became the pitcher of choice. It made me nervous to be man in charge, but after the first pitch, I was okay. I was slender and could not throw very fast so the opposing team would score as our fielders were not too skilled. My dad showed me how to hold the ball with it clamped tightly with the ball of my thumb against my fingers and to snap it to spin as I released it. I soon learned how to throw and control a big round house side arm curve ball. Most batters would hold up and not swing at the first few balls as many pitchers had poor control and they would be walked. However, I would get 2 strikes on them right away and I would throw my curve ball. Many had never seen a curve ball and would jump back as the ball would curve across the plate for a strike. One man usually umpired behind the plate. One father of one of the boys kept the records and made sure that the box score and a write-up was in the next issue of the Red Cloud newspaper. Mom kept a lot of the newspaper clippings and put them in my scrapbook. Out of the 3 years that I played, she saved 25 clippings of the games. The one clipping shows that I pitched a shut out and we won the game 6 to 0. Another where we won and I struck out 16 batters in the 7 innings that we played. We had just received our new caps and uniforms. Another clipping was when we played across the state line in Lebanon, Kansas and had good press. It was during the summer anniversary celebration and was well attended. Our regular catcher was not able to play so we had an excellent player step in. A good catcher sure made it a lot easier. Most games were with towns in Nebraska. We played a game in Hastings that is a much larger town. We lost but fans made comments about my good pitching and applauded when I came up to bat. That pleased me. Being a farm boy who moved to town was difficult. Having the chance to play baseball and excel did more than anything to help my self-esteem as I always felt insecure. My reputation as a pitcher spread more than I realized at the time. The coach in the small town of Cowles north of Red Cloud had a relative who was a scout for the then Brooklyn Dodgers. He met my dad and I one Sunday in town and wanted to see me pitch. We went down to Hedge field and I threw pitch after pitch. He asked me to try different things. One was to thrown move overhand and not so much side arm or partial overhand. I tried to do as he said. Then we sat at the counter in the café and talked. He finally said that he could okay a train trip to Florida to try out for the minor leagues. Dad did not to influence me one way or the other. It was too big of a step and I made the decision not to go.

Of course one always wonders. It taught me that practice and persistence pay off. I never knew how pitching for hours and hours to improve would impact me later in life.

My mother saved clippings from the newspaper of the games I played in. There were 25 in my scrapbook from the 3 seasons that I played. Of the 5 that I chose, one was where I had struck out 13 in the 7-inning game, another where we had our new uniforms and caps and I pitched a shut out. Another where the Hastings folks made nice comments and applauded when I came to bat. We lost the game but we were outgunned. We played the one game in Lebanon, KS and I was the only kid that went to Nebraska high school rather than Lebanon from that era. The short clipping noted that we played the one high school game.

Red Cloud Juniors Defeat Lebanon Juniors
(By Frank Sidlo)

Friday evening, July 15th, the Red Cloud Junior Legion defeated the Lebanon Junior Legion by a score of 10-2 in a very good game played at Lebanon, Kansas. Saturday they will play Smith Center, Kansas, winners of the Thursday game in a tournament held during the Homecoming celebration at Lebanon, Kansas.

Stones for the first time could cut loose with everything he had, having Moranville of Guide Rock behind the plate about whom a lot of praise was heard all around on his style of catching. And what a job of catching he did, especially those one-handed stops. Stones was at his best, allowing only 2 hits and both of them came in the 5th inning when Lebanon scored their two runs. In the first four innings, only 12 men came to bat. Phifer was an outstanding fielder of the evening, followed closely by Eddy. A good crowd of fans was on hand to see this game.

The box score:

Red Cloud Juniors

	AB	R	H	PO	A
Haresnape 2b	3	2	0	1	0
Killough ss	3	2	0	0	3
Kelliher ss	0	0	0	0	0
Phifer 3b	3	1	0	3	2
Moranville c	4	2	1	3	2
Sprague rf	1	1	0	0	0
Richardson lf	3	0	1	0	0
Beardslee cf	2	1	0	0	0
Eddy 1b	2	1	0	6	0
Stones p	2	0	0	0	1
Totals	23	10	2	21	8

Lebanon Juniors

	AB	R	H	PO	A
Anthony c	3	0	0	7	1
Heaston 1b	3	0	0	7	0
Deschant ss	3	0	0	1	1
Isom cf	2	0	0	1	0
Beardslee 2b p	3	1	1	1	3
x Bloomer p lf	3	1	0	1	1
Camp 3b	3	0	1	1	1
Post lf	2	0	0	1	1
May rf	2	0	0	0	0
Totals	24	2	2	21	8

x Bloomer relieved Beardslee in 5th inning with one out.

Score by innings:

Red Cloud .... 300 331 0—10
Lebanon 000 020 0 2

Summary: Errors, Killough 1, Sprague 1, Bloomer 2, Deschant 1. Earned runs, Red Cloud 7, Lebanon 1. Runs batted in, Haresnape 1, Moranville 4, Richardson 3, Eddy 1, Camp 2. 2 base hits, Camp 1. Bases on balls, off Stones, 1 in 7 innings; off Beardslee, 5 in 4 1-3 innings; off Bloomer, 2 in 2 2-3 innings. Stolen bases, Haresnape 3, Killough 1, Moranville 2, Eddy 1. Strike outs, by Stones, 7 in 7 innings; by Beardslee, 6 in 4 1-3 innings; by Bloomer, 1 in 2 2-3 innings. Hits off Stones, 2 in 7 innings; off Beardslee, 2 in 4 1-3 innings. Hit by pitched ball, by Beardslee, Killough 1, Sprague 1. Wild pitch, Beardslee 1. Passed balls, Anthony 1. Left on base, Red Cloud 1, Lebanon 2. Winning pitcher, Stones. Losing pitcher, Beardslee. Umpires, Fair and Coulson. Time of game, 1 hour, 18 minutes.

Red Cloud High Athletes Participating In Track and Baseball This Spring

RED CLOUD, (TNS) — Red Cloud high athletes are participating in two interscholastic sports this spring—track and baseball.

Coach Dick Borton is directing both sports.

LOOKS TO SOPHOMORES

Red Cloud is in its second year of track following a year layoff. Borton says he doesn't have too much in the way of prospects but adds that a large sophomore turnout augurs well for a team in a year or two.

T. Mason is the only track letterman. He and K. Pitney are sprinters. J. Soderlain and A. Phifer will run the hurdles. L. Stokes, G. Stokes, C. Beardslee and R. Farrar are ticketed for the distances and B. Knigge, J. Eddy and L. Grewell will handle the weights.

Red Cloud has played one baseball game, a 9-2 win over Riverton, and has tilts scheduled with Nelson at Red Cloud April 19, Riverton at Red Cloud April 26 and Nelson at Nelson May 9. More games may be added, Borton said.

STRIKES OUT 12

In the Riverton game, Stone, Red Cloud hurler, fanned 12. Phifer clouted three for three and Knigge and Arneson smacked doubles. Colley chucked for the losers.

Deshler Passes Up Track Program

DESHLER, (TNS)—Lack of interest has led Deshler high school to pass up track and field competition this spring. Baseball may be played if the weather is suitable. Deshler is a member of the Big Eight Conference.

Hastings Juniors Win Over Red Cloud
(By Frank Sidlo)

Wednesday evening, June 21, the Red Cloud Juniors journeyed to Hastings only to come out on the short end by a score of 3-1 in a well played game. This was another pitcher's duel, taking place at the beautiful Duncan Field.

The game started promptly at 8 p.m. Only two extra base hits were scored, one for Hart, a two base hit, and Phifer, a three base hit. This was the only hit given up by Hupf. The five hits given up by Stones went to: Hart 2, Garber 2, Marr 1, and from the comment received from the Hastings fans after the game, Stones put on the best exhibition of pitching so far this season at Duncan Field. This was evident from the applause he drew from the fans when going to bat.

The box score:

Red Cloud

	ab	r	h	po	a
Haresnape ss	4	0	0	1	1
McEntee 3b	4	1	0	1	1
Knigge c	4	0	0	12	0
Phifer 2b	4	0	1	2	2
Courtright rf	2	0	0	0	0
Sidlo cf	3	0	0	0	0
Stones p	4	0	0	0	3
Eddy 1b	3	0	0	5	0
Hubbard lf	3	0	0	2	0
Farrar lf	0	0	0	1	0
Totals	31	1	1	24	7

Hastings

	ab	r	h	po	a
Garber rf	3	3	2	2	0
Gillespie 1b	4	0	0	7	1
Hart ss	3	0	2	1	3
Bonifas lf	3	0	0	0	0
Marsh cf	4	0	0	1	0
Marr 3b	4	0	1	0	1
Paulson 2b	3	0	0	4	1
Perdue c	1	0	0	12	0
Hupf p	4	0	0	0	2
Totals	29	3	5	27	8

Score by innings:

Red Cloud .... 000 001 000—1
Hastings .... 101 000 10x—3

Summary: Errors, Hubbard, McEntee, Haresnape, Hart 2, Gillespie. Runs batted in, Bonifas 2, Hart. Stolen bases, Phifer 2, Courtright, McEntee, Garber 5, Hart. Two base hits, Hart 1. Three base hits, Phifer 1. Bases on balls, off Stones 8, Hupf 2. Hits off Stones 5, off Hupf 1. Sacrifice hits, Bonifas 1. Strike outs, by Stones 12, Hupf 12. Hit by pitcher, by Stones, Sidlo. Earned runs, Hastings 2. Passed balls, Knigge 1, Perdue 1. Left on base, Red Cloud 6, Hastings 11. Winning pitcher, Hupf. Losing pitcher, Stones. Umpires, Glen McQueston, plate, Carlos

Red Cloud Juniors Defeat Blue Hill Juniors
(By Frank Sidlo)

Friday evening at Hedge Field, the Red Cloud Junior Legion nine initiated their new uniforms by defeating the Blue Hill Junior Legion by a score of 6-2. Rocky was a master of the mound for the Red Cloud Juniors, by striking out 16 batters in 7 innings. In the fifth and sixth innings, with the bases loaded and only one out, he showed his mastery by striking out the next two batters to put an end to the Blue Hill Juniors' rally. This gave Red Cloud fans quite a thrill and something to talk about. Was it the new uniforms that had something to do with winning the game? Anyway the lads took more like ball players in their creams trimmed with dark blue uniforms and dark blue caps to match. One could not help to notice how proud the lads were when they trotted out on the field. And don't forget too, their manager was just as proud or perhaps even more so; thanks to ... in ... Cloud ... ... coming up Indians ... tomorrow.

A nice crowd of spectators was on hand to see this game. Some Guide Rock fans were also noted among the crowd. Come again boys, you are always welcome.

The next league game will be at Blue Hill next Friday, July 30th. Any of you fans wanting to see the boys in action, come to Blue Hill Friday. Take in the home coming celebration and watch the game in the afternoon. On August 1st, the Juniors go to Lawrence. This is another league game and don't forget, Wednesday night's game when the Detroit Senators will come to Red Cloud to play under the lights against the Indians.

The box score:

Red Cloud Juniors

	AB	R	H	O	A	E
Phifer, 2b	4	1	1	2	1	1
Sidlo, lf	4	3	1	0	0	0
Sprague, 1b	4	1	2	2	0	1
Day, 3b	3	1	1	0	0	0
Pope, c	2	0	0	15	2	1
Killough, ss	4	0	0	0	0	0
Beardslee, cf	2	0	1	0	0	0
Eddy, rf	2	0	0	1	0	1
Anderson, rf	1	0	0	0	0	0
Stones, p	2	0	0	1	0	0
Totals	28	6	6	21	3	4

Blue Hill Juniors

	AB	R	H	O	A	E
Putz, ss	4	0	1	2	0	0
McConkey, 2b	1	1	0	0	1	...
Sabrass, 2b	2	0	1	0	2	0
Heppen, c	4	1	0	10	1	1
Post, 3b	4	0	1	1	0	0
Bachman, 1b	3	0	0	5	0	3
Marquardt, lf	3	0	0	0	0	0
Brows, cf	2	0	0	0	0	0
Anderson, rf	2	0	0	0	0	0
Knigge, rf	1	0	0	0	0	0
Kort, p	3	0	1	0	4	0
Totals	30	2	4	18	8	4

x Knigge batted for Anderson in the sixth inning.

Score by innings:

Blue Hill .... 200 000 0—2
Red Cloud .... 310 101 x—6

Summary: Errors, Phifer 1, ..., Heppen 1, Bachman 3; earned runs, Red Cloud 6, Blue Hill 1; runs batted in, Sprague 2, Day 2, Pope 1, Post 1; two base hit, Day 1; stolen base, Phifer 1, Sidlo (home), Sprague 1, Day 1; bases on balls, Day 1, Pope 1, Beardslee 1, Stones 1, McConkey 1, Knigge 1; hits off Stones, 4 in 7 innings, off Kort, 6 in 6 innings; strike outs, by Stones, 16 in 7 innings, by Kort, 9 in 6 innings; hit by pitched ball, by Kort, Pope; left on bases, Red Cloud 8, Blue Hill 8; umpires, Fair, balls and strikes, McMahon, bases; time of game, 2 hours, 10 minutes.

first man up out, pitcher to first; second, catcher to first; third struck out, thus ending their inning. This one inning really had the fans a howling. Too bad such a small crowd was on hand to see this game. Fans, you missed a good ball game and a lot of laughs.

Try to turn out for their next home game, June the 27th, when the Lawrence Juniors visit our city. Remember, Nelson comes to Red Cloud on the same date to cross bats with the Indians. The Junior game will followed the Nelson-Red Cloud game, if not changed to a night game. Announcement will be made before the Nelson-Red Cloud tilt. Let's keep the date in mind and give the Juniors a real turnout.

The box score:

Franklin

	AB	R	H	O	A	E
Spargo, c	3	0	1	0	1	1
Smolley, ss	3	0	1	1	2	1
Long, 3b	3	0	1	1	6	3
Gregory, cf	3	0	0	0	0	0
McKee, 2b	1	0	0	4	0	0
Slocum, 1b	3	0	0	7	0	1
Diener, lf	3	0	0	1	0	0
Folkers, rf	2	0	0	0	0	0
Harbolt, p	2	0	0	2	1	0
Totals	23	0	3	16	10	6

Red Cloud

	AB	R	H	O	A	E
Phifer, 2b	3	1	0	1	0	0
D. Gleason, ss	3	0	0	1	4	0
B. Gleason, 3b	2	2	2	0	1	0
Pope, c	2	1	1	0	1	0
Day, lf, 1b	3	1	1	1	0	0
Sidlo, lf	2	0	1	0	0	0
Killough, ss	2	0	0	1	0	0
Henderson, rf	2	0	0	0	0	0
Stones, p	3	0	1	0	2	1
Sprague, 1b	0	1	0	5	0	0
Beardslee, cf	1	0	0	0	0	0
Eddy, rf	1	0	0	0	0	0
Totals	24	6	5	9	8	1

Score by innings:

Franklin	000 000 0—0
Red Cloud	102 003 x—6

Summary: Errors, Stones 1, Spargo 1, Smolley 1, Long 3, Slocum 1; two base hits, B. Gleason 1, Day 1; stolen base, B. Gleason, Pope, Sprague, Stones, Spargo, McKee; hit by pitcher, by Harbolt, Sprague; bases on balls, off Harbolt, Phifer, B. Gleason, Pope, off Stones, McKee 2; strike outs, by Stones 10, by Harbolt 3; runs batted in, B. Gleason 1, Pope 1, Day 1; earned runs, Red Cloud 3; double play, Gleason to Sprague, Smolley to McKee to Slocum; hits off Stones, 3 in 6 innings, Harbolt 5 in 7 innings; wild pitch, Harbolt 3; left on bases, Red Cloud 8, Franklin 4; winning pitcher, Stones; losing pitcher, Harbolt; umpires, Barrows and Fair, strikes and balls, Pope, bases; time, 1 hour, 40 minutes.

I especially remember playing the small town of Guide Rock just east of Red Cloud. Those boys had been well coached and we were badly beaten the first two times we played by 15 or 16 to one. Our last game ended 6 to 5 which was not bad but I sure wanted to finally win one from them. They would stand in and wait for the curve ball and were ready. One time I had gone to Franklin, NE to swim on a hot summer day and pitched that night. My curve ball was not working well as I was very tired. One cocky batter stood there waiting for the ball to break and then realized it was heading right for him. He swung around and the ball hit him in the lower back and he fell to the ground, I was afraid I had injured him, but he was able to take his base. He was more watchful after that. Only his pride was injured.

Another time, he would steal base after base. If I would turn and throw to first he would make it second as our players could not throw and catch well enough. If I threw to second he would scoot back to first. In the same way he would steal third from second. One time when he was on second and took a big lead, I turned to throw and he took off for third thinking I was going to throw to second. Instead I threw to our shortstop who was a pretty good player. The runner was startled and tried to stop and run back to second but slipped and fell down. The shortstop just had to reach down and tag him for the out. Our coach enjoyed that play. I do not know why I thought of that throw, but it worked perfectly and saved face as he was making us look silly.

J.T.

Introduction

James Timothy Stones was born on September 30, 1828 in Zanesville, Ohio, Morgan County and Bloom Township. He left Ohio when he was 12 years of age. The 1850 census shows JT in Waynesville, Illinois, Dewitt County (age 22). He married Mary Morehead from Tazewell County, Illinois on October 4, 1855 (age 27). He moved to northwest Missouri in 1864 (age 36) and finally to Smith County, Kansas in 1874 (age 46) where he homesteaded land and lived until his death on July 17, 1899 at the age of 70.

How JT received his education is unknown, but his writing indicates an educated person. He was on the roles of the Methodist Episcopal Church of Missouri while moving across the state as a minister. In his letters he refers to his work as a minister with a parsonage and income he received. When he moved to Kansas, he was removed from the Missouri records. The Methodist Church was not yet organized in Kansas. He donated several acres of land for a church and cemetery on the northeast corner of the homestead of 160 acres. Few of his sons and grandsons have been involved in the ministry. My dad was named Cornelius Alonzo. These names came from the bible. Cornelius was a Roman centurion. He and his family became the first Gentiles to be baptized in the name of Jesus Christ. Alonzo was a favorite name for my grandmother as it was the name of her favorite brother. Dad attended funerals and one of my bible class programs. One year a missionary, his wife and daughter came and had summer bible school. The daughter played the accordion that I enjoyed. We had parts to memorize and go up front and speak them. The boys were told to not put their hands in their pockets. I was too young to remember but the audience was amused as I put both of my hands on top of my head. I still remember the song we sang. I will make you fishers of men if you will follow me.

When my mother moved from Colorado to the farm, she became involved in the Mt Hope Club or women's group at the church. On Sunday she would wake me and we would walk the one half mile east to the church. She never learned to drive and dad never attended. That was his time to rest after hard farm work the week before. Mom would put a roast on the stove and it was dad's job to make sure the fire did not go out while we were gone. What a great aroma when we returned. If it was wet and muddy we would wear overshoes as the road was slick. There was no full time minister so we just had Sunday school classes. One cousin would call the meeting to order and take care of business items like ordering new quarterly books or other matters and then began classes. The adult class was led by one cousin and met on the south side of the room about halfway back. Across the room on the north side was where the older youth met. Mom would teach the cradle role of young children at the front of the church. The teacher would take attendance and hold out the quarterly and collect the offering. The younger students got to pick the last hymn and stand in front as they sang. When years were good, we would have a visiting minister who would come occasionally and preach a sermon. One older lady cousin would give the closing prayer. As she got older, the prayers got longer and longer. It was difficult for the younger ones especially to remain still.

I have many memories of the church. My cousins who lived close to the church would start a fire in the furnace when it was cold. I helped once and went into the basement where the furnace was located. The heated air rose into the church above through a metal register. It felt nice to stand on the grill and let the warm air take away the chill on a cold day. In the steeple there was a bell that we would ring with the rope that hung down. By the time people arrived the room would be warm. I attended my grandfather's funeral. The casket was wheeled in through the double doors below the steeple. A Methodist minister came from town to lead the service. One song was "The Old Rugged Cross." A quartet sang some special music.

The building was typical of a church. The floor was sloped from back to front. There were wooden seats that raise and lower with a center section and aisles on either side with seats. There was a raised section in front with a podium in the center and two large chairs with stuffed seats covered with leather on either side. The piano was behind that with chairs in a semicircle for the choir. One of the small stained glass windows had "In honor of J T Stones and wife." It was removed when the building was renovated and I still possess it.

Ohio

Zanesville is in Muskingum County and is famous for the "Y" bridge in the middle of the city. The bridge spans the Licking and Muskingum rivers. In 1797, Ebenezer Zane and a party of woodmen cut a path from Wheeling through the Ohio forest to Maysville, Kentucky. Dubbed "Zane's Trace," this path became a gateway to the rich lands of the west. Ferries were operated to cross the major rivers and river travel was important in the early years.

The 1810 census of Washington County, Newport Township shows James Stones. The household consisted of one male under 10, one between 26 and 45, two females under 10 and one between 16 and 26. The 1820 census shows Samuel Stones in Washington County. In 1830, James, Samuel and Thomas Stones are shown. Thomas is in Morgan County, Bloom Township with a male and female between 20 and 30 and a male under 5 years of age that would fit JT's age since he was born in 1828. In the 1840 census, Thomas Stones is in Muskingum county, Zanesville town with a male and female between 30 and 40, a male between 10 and 15, one between 5 and 10 and one under 5 and a female between 15 and 20. This closely matches JT's siblings in a later census except for the older female. Marriage records show that Thomas Stones and Joanna Edwards were married on October 4, 1827 in Morgan County, Ohio

Illinois

In 1850, Dewitt county, Waynesville town, the census shows Joannah G. Stones, 42 with James, 22, Homer C., 17, William, 11 and Thomas H., 5. 1880 shows Joannah G., 72 in McLean county, McLean city with Nelle G.D. (grand daughter) 12, Thomas H., 46, Elvira, 30, and Charles H., 9. No spouse is mentioned for Joannah in the 1850 census records. She married John Longworth on December 22, 1881 in McLean, Illinois at age 73. Her parents were John Edwards B. Feb 5, 1770 D. Aug 6, 1842 Mt. Hope, McLean, Ill, and Judith Cross B. Aug 19, 1771 Salisbury, Essex, Mass, D Oct 27, 1842 Mt. Hope, McLean, Ill.

Mary Morehead was born in 1830 and Emigrated to America Monroe County, Ohio from Ireland between 1834 and 1837. She moved to Tazewell County, Illinois in 1854, one year before marrying JT. They left Illinois around 1864 for Missouri. She died on July 25, 1907 in Smith County, Kansas.

JT's youngest brother, Thomas H served in the army during the Civil War or War Between the States. He was 18 years old when he mustered in on September 19, 1862 at Camp Butler, Springfield, Illinois. He was 5 feet, 6 ½ inches tall with hazel eyes, dark complexion and black hair. His occupation was given as farmer and was a private in Company A of the 117 Illinois Infantry. He was on the campaigns to Meridian, Miss, Red River, LA, Oxford, Miss, Tupelo, Miss, Missouri after Price Tennessee after Hood and Alabama. Was in the battle of Fort DeRussy and Pleasant Hill, La, Tupelo, Miss, Nashville, Tennessee and Blakely, Alabama. Mustered out at Camp Butler, Ill August 5, 1865. A Declaration for Pension was made on the 12th day of October 1920 McLean, Ill, when he was 76 years of age. He was born at Mt Hope Township, McLean County, Ill. on March 30, 1844. His height was given as 5 feet, 8 inches with fair complexion when he was honorably discharged. Reason for pension request is that he has rheumatism - is absolutely helpless and requires the constant attention of wife and friends. Has not been out of house for a year. While on the Meredian Raid, State of Mississippi on or about the 15th or 20th day of March 1864 from exposure and drinking impure water he contracted affection of the eyes and Gravel. He was treated on Hospital Boat, Thomas E. Lutt. He was listed as a Wheelwright and Wagon Maker and ran the Stone and Wood blacksmith shop in McLean with a man by the name of Wood. He died on Feb 11, 1921 and is buried in the McLean cemetery west of the city. He married Elvira (Elmina) Cunningham on Jan 1, 1867 in McLean, Illinois.

Mary Morehead's parents were Wm Sr. born about March 26, 1803. He died May 28, 1879 at the age of 76 yrs, 2 mo, and 2 days and Elizabeth who died 10-4-1868. Alexander was born on May 28, 1828 and died in 1850, Mary on Nov 28, 1829and died in 1907, John on Dec 20, 1834, Margrat on Aug 20, 1836 and died in 1837, James on April 25, 1839 and Margrat on Oct 18, 1842 and died in 1843.

Missouri

With a team and wagon, JT, Mary, and children Lyman, Laura and Nellie traveled west. They crossed the Illinois River at Pekin, Ill., a week later crossed the Mississippi river and a week later arrived in Chillicothe, Mo. JT joined the Missouri Conference and took a circuit in Eagleville, Harrison County, Mo. in 1865. In October 1867, they were in Bancroft, Davis County, Mo. In 1868, they are in Edinburg and in 1869 in Proctorvill. Rolla and Zell were born in Missouri.

Kansas

JT moved to Kansas in 1874 where he homesteaded land. Homestead Certificate No. 3064, Application 6915 of the land office at Kirwin, Kansas states the Act of Congress approved 20th May, 1862 " To secure Homesteads to actual Settlers on the Public Domain" for the northeast quarter of section seventeen in township one, of range eleven, in the district of lands subject to sale at Kirwin, Kansas containing one hundred and sixty acres. The certificate is dated the first day of November 1880 by President Rutherford B. Hayes. Recorded in Volume 6 Page 430. JT also obtained a timber claim. Timber Culture Certificate No. 117, Application 198. Acts of Congress approved March 3, 1873, March 13, 1874 and June 14, 1878 "To encourage the Growth of Timber on the Western Prairies" for the southeast quarter of section eight in township one south of range eleven west of the sixth principal meridian containing one hundred and sixty acres. Dated the ninth day of April 1887. Recorded Vol. 4, Page 251 and filed Dec 9, 1891 at the Land Office in Kirwin, Kansas.

In a letter written to his mother, Joanna G. Stones at McLean, Ill., dated July 6, 1879, he tells of "building a house 16X26 with an ell 14X20 one story under the ground a basement the ell for a cellar the basement is rock on the basement. I will put a fraim 16X26 one story and a half on the ell one story giving us counting the cellar ten rooms."

Letters

From the time JT left Illinois until he was settled in Kansas, he wrote letters to his mother, Joanna. The first is dated Nov 23rd 1865 and the last January 30, 1881. Charles O. Stones was working in the school system in Hugoton, Kansas in the 1970s. The druggist there said that his wife's mother had been a Stones and she had some old letters. When Joanna G. Stones had died, this lady had gone back to Illinois or received the trunk that contained the letters and Charles was able to make copies of the letters that his Great Grandfather had written and send them to me in February 1980. They make very interesting reading and give some answers, but also raise many questions. From 1869 to 1878, there are no letters, otherwise they are written every year or so. The following is the contents of the letters:

Eagleville No 23rd 1865 Mother, I have found a stoping place at last in the above named place, Harrison Co. Mo that is for the winter. I intend to go on in the spring. I got scared at the emigration to Kansas this fall. Hok went on to Kansas and came back and staid one night with us and then went on. He says that Kansas is the place. Corn is worth ten cents per pound, hay fourteen dollars per tun, eight dollars per day for man and team so it goes. Well, we are living in this town with a sister of Uncle John Browns of Macaknaw, a fine family. We are all well. I gess Lyman has not got here. We have been keping house one week. My house and wood does not cost me any thing but the wood hauling. Every thing but meet is plenty, it is high. Every thing els is reasonable, land rates from 2.50 to 5.00 per acre, this is wild land improved lands are in proportion. Well we had a hard time to get here. The mud was awfull. We camped in our wagon every night but one and that was in Pekin untill we got to John Gibsons in Chilicothe. We have been to all the acquaintances in this country. I saw Uncle John stones. He intends to go to Kansas in the spring. I do not regret leaving Ill. if I do not go any farther. I find lots of folks here that I knowed scattered all over this country. We miss our cow badly. The cows have gon dry so that they are hard to get now. Tell Dick that I left his money with James Moorhead 32 dollars and then 15 he owed me and 1.50 with David Carr and 1.50 with Henry Leasures making (50) fifty dollars the amount I owed him, I believe. It is late in the afternoon and Mary wants the table to get super and I must close by subscribing myself, yours as ever James Stones. Direct to Eaglevill Harrison Co. Mo. Mary says my remark about Lyman is rather blank. We are looking for him to day in the stage from Bethany Mo. (Words were scribbled around JT's signature-perhaps Thomas H Stones practicing writing and copying Stones and James T)

Eagleville March 2, 1866. Mother. I take this morning to write you a brief note to answer yours. I do not know that I can answer all of your inquiries having lost your letter. You asked for the particulars of our trip. There was nothing special about it but mud which came near killing my horses, especialy buck. We crosed the Ill river on Wednesday morning. The next Wednesday morning we crost the Miss river and the following Wednesday we reached Chilicothe where we met John. We visited all the acquaintances all around looking at the country and then went on to this circuit this winter where we are at this date in good health with plenty of good hearty vituals. Well pleased with the people of this circuit. The are not willing for us to go on to Kansas, but insist on our joining the Conference which I have consented to do conditionally. I shall wait untill I hear from Conf. If I receive an appointment I will stay in Mo, if not I will go on to Kansas about the midle of this month. Homer will load up about the 8th and leave. Charly has been very sick this winter with a tonsil affection. We thought he would die for several day but they are all well at this date. I have one hundred dollars for my winter work. My little mare died about the last of January. I have been offered forty acres of improved land for buck. This is a very broken country. Nothing near as good a farming country as Ill. Tell D-that if he goes to Kansas to be shure to hunt me up. I intend to go to Kansas this summer at all events and buy a peace of land for a home. I have nothing of importance to write. Lyman fell on the ice this winter and cut his cheek badly which has left a very bad scar which I am afraid will injure his looks as long as he lives. Nettie is the greatest hand for corn bread I ever saw. Laura is rather poorly this winter. Write soon and often. We remain yours as ever, James Stones. (Included with the letter was a picture with writing "Residence of James Moorhead" and "This is a picture of our house. I wish you could come and see us." There was also the words "Thomas H Stones" written twice and Thomas scratched out on the top of the first page)

The following letter(s) is/are signed Mary Stones and is/are not nearly as well written as JTs.

The 12 Eagleville March. Dear Mother. I take my pen in hand to let you know that we are all well at present. We was glad to hear from you all. We was surprised to hear that Dick was married but was glad to know that he done so well. Tell them I wish them a long and happy life. We are pleased with the likenes that they sent us. The children make a great fuss about it and have to look at it every day and show it to every won that comes in. Tell them later to write to us often. We was disapointed about Father. We looked for him every Saturday till last Saturday. We got a letter from him and he said he will come soon. O how I would like to see you all and have a good time again. I think I could spend a month visiting in McLain. I would like to see Miss Glotpilter and all the rest of my old neighbors. I think I will try and come in the fall if we all are well. I want to see uncle John and family sow bad and I want to see the…..all the rest…..Homer was …..i would be glad. It makes me feel sad to leave him. In……and among strangers. We got a letter from Hok Saturday. They are all well. Hannah sais she never knew what hard times was before. Write often Mother. Mary Stones.

Laura and Lyman is goin too school all the time. The learn fast. Laura reeds in the fourth reader and Lyman in the third. Laura is learning to write fast. Nettie is growing very fast. She is fat, sasy and hearty. We spoil her as she is the baby. Know you you wanted to know how I got along when the bab was born. Well I had a very hard time after the babe was born. Worse then when Lyman was born. You know how I got along then. I think I worked to hard. I ….and maid about thirty yards of cloth. I maid too …and some …and….. I did not get my ….till I moved west and I was very poorly all the time. I had no epetite to eat. James is away from home at present. He is holden a big meeten at battle creek. We have had some very good meetens this winter. He does not no what he will do yet. He did not go to conference but I think he will travel if the give him a work. We will know inn a few dais as conference is goin on now. I am encious to know where we will go. James will write and tell you where to write as soon as we know. Now Mother I don't want you to let eny body see this. It is spelled so bad and so hasty evian I don't think you can read half of it as it is. Third letter that I have tried since I came to Missouri. James is hurring mee too go with himto his Appointment and I must stop. I am not very strong yet. I feel lonsome. I miss you both so much Now. Mother iff you can reed this I will write to you soon. Nothing More at present. Yours as ever Mary Stones

Eagleville Dec 4th/66. Mother. I this moment take pen to write you a few lines in order that you may know that we are still in the land of the living. We are all well at present and pretty comfortably situated. The children have good home made clothing. Mary has a good flannel dress for winter. Nettie is so big and fat you would not know her. Hearty as a bear. Laura's health is much better than it was in Ill. I have nothing of importance to write as I am in this land of strangers to you. They are kind and we are not home sick. We had rather be poor here than there as we can...........I should like very much to see you and all the rest of the folks and will probably come to see you in the course of time. I have received but two letters from Hok since he left here. The last letter said they had all been sick this fall but all war about again. I do not know what I shall do as I do not think I will travel. I hear that Lattie and Susan are about comeing together again. I hope you will have nothing to do with them. Lett them go for what they will fetch. Keep clear of them. About the time you get this my Elder will be passing through your town. We have no chance to get our likeness taken at present but will send them at the first opportunity. I believe I have written all I have worth of writing and will close as it is getting late at night. Our third qtr meeting ...... the first and second of the month. Philo Baldwing has left Mo and gon to Ill. Write soon and often to your children is the wish of you Son James Stones. (Mary adds a few lines) Well Mother as James did not tell you about our babe I will tell you. It was born the first of November and died the twentieth. It was .....little boy. It seemed healthy for about too weeks and then it took sick. We did not know what ailed it it. We caled it William tomes.

Bancroft Oct 22nd/67. Dear Mother. I set down to drop you a hasty note saying we are all well at present but I have lost my voice so that I am fearfull that I shall never recover it. I have a large scope of country to travel over and thirteen appointments and two years studieng to do this year. I expect to brake down if I do I shall go on to Kansas in the spring instead of visiting Ill. Father was out to see us this fall I recon he come after fire. I have not heard from Homer for some time. They ware well last I heard. The children are going to school. Laura is reeding the 5th reader writeing and ciphering. Lyman is reading in the 3 reader and studing Rays mental arithmetic. Net is the greatest gal you ever saw. A sensible child shure. Our pretracted meeting commences Friday night in town. The last letter we got from you come to Edinburg and we did not get it for a month or two after its arrival. The people of Mo can stand bombadment by the Gospel artillery the longest and the most affectual of any place I ever saw. I am getting a support. Nothing more at present. Write soon and often. Yours as ever James Stones. (Written upside down at the top of the first page "Direct to Bancroft Davis Co Mo. The envelope shows a 3 cent stamp "Xed" out and addressed to: Mrs. J. G. Stones, McLane, McLane Co Ill. and at the top "Bancroft Mo Oct 25, 1867."

Bancroft Feb 13th 1868. Dear Grand Ma I take my pen in hand to Write you a few lines to let you know I am well and I am trying to learn read Wright and Spell. Tell Uncle I want to see the bab. I wanted to come so bad I have not been going to school this winter. I want to see you so bad. Write soon. Write me a letter. Miss Laura Ann stones.

Edinburg Nov 17th 1868. Dear Mother. I seat myself this cold blustry morning to adress you a few lines. We are all well at preasent. Mary and the children arrived at home safe and sound. We got our things through safe. We have not heard a word from hoke sense we come home. I intend to write to him today. I got a letter from Dadson lately. They are well and boarding at Jack Fosters: Pella, is their Post Office. We are living in a tolerably comefortable house this winter. Tell Dick my dog is as spry as a cat and promises to be a fine hunter. Mary wants to know how the baby mouth has got. Dick the Hickry nuts ware all gon when I got home. Thare was no big ones this year and but few little ones. If you want to by a piece of land now is the time. You can buy the choice for ten dollars an acre. The children are going to school. We are very much behind with our preparations for winter because of our visit to Ill but I think we will get up yet. I am about starting to a two days meeting in connection with our Quarterly meeting at Spring Hill twenty miles distant. I wish you would come and pay us a visit this winter or in the Spring. I have an agency for professor Smiths Bible Dictionary, it is a noble work. Nettie talks about Grandma a great deal and wants you to come out here. My trip cost me over one hundred dollars but I do not regret it Hoping you will write soon and often. I will close by subscribeing myself yours as ever. James T Stones.

Proctorvill May the 25th 1869. Dear Mother. After weeks and perhaps months delay I set down to write you a few lines. We are all well at present and comfortably situated on Proctorvill circuit in a very parsonage with a small work of six appointments with a salary of five hundred dollars over and above the house and fire wood. We have had some five meetings last fall and winter and this spring. We have a good church here and generaly a large congregation. Laura, Lyman and Nettie are going to school now. We expect to go to Edinburgh in the course of two or three weeks on a visit to see the friends we labored with two years so pleasantly. I expect we will have a nice time. I wish you was here to go with us. We have a good many friends up there. I have not got but one letter from Homer sense we come home from Ill. I intend to go and see him this summer and I think you might come out and go with me. It is only about one hundred and twenty miles from here. This is the twenty seventh. Maggie is one year old today. She has twelve teeth and can runn whure ever she please in the house or yard. Our association meets soon and I have not my essay written yet. We have not had any mail for three weeks. I expect it will come today sonsequently I will finish up a half doz letters. My time is very much taken up with the lay congregation question at present and hope it will be a failure though I bet it will be adopted. Now write often and tell us all the news. We have nothing in this land of strangers to write that would interest you as you have. Tell us about Dick and family, Enos and family, Marion Dave Uncles Jacob, John and all the rest of the folks. Tell them to write to us. I believe I have writen all I have to write at present and will close for the time being by subscribe myself. yours as ever James T Stones.

Mt. Hope Kans Oct 21, 1878. Dear Mother. I received your letter beareing sad inteligence of the Death of Aunt G Cousins. I have to send you the sad fact that Lauras daughter Clara died Oct 18, 1878 Aged one year and 18 days. Truly in life we are in the midst of death. I learned by Father ..... Tidd that Aunt Moore was not expected to live. You said nothing about her in your letter. We are in good health yet there has been a good deal of sickness here this fall. Mary got hurt a week or two ago by the ash gum falling on her. Yes, the banner of holiness comes tolerably regular. You ask me what I think of it. Perhaps I had better not spend my opinions to freely. Holiness is a Bible doctrin. Holiness begets a spirit of humility rather than a spirit of boasting. I think the free Methodist in this country are to bashfull. I think a man ought to be arefull to posess what he profess. I am like Mag Presham. A great many of the sanctified ones I am afraid of. Bill Rayburn for instance and Mrs Inskip of Baltimore. Enough of this. We have plenty to eat. Times are very hard here. Mony is almost out of the Question. Wheat the Best Quality. 4 Oct we thrashed 356 bushels. You said nothing about that Estate. I recon it is lost. We shall never get any of it. I supose Dick is still wagon making. What is your best wagon worth. Eastern wagons are selling here for from 70 to 90 dollars. The price of everything is down down. Certainly times must get better soon. Our winter School will commence soon. I will close soon for my pen is poor. My ink is gon. Good night Ma. J.T.Stones. (Some writing in another hand: Many thanks my Bros. For your kindness. Many thanks Dear Bro..for your Kind attention advising me of the whereabouts of my my .... Cousins F.B. T Azihcraft Evangelists..I think they with some others loved ones, would come here and hold a convention that these hordes of sinners & half harted professers might get waked up & git loved & ... loved for which my Lord is all a blaze. You ask Jesus about it.)

Red Cloud July 6th 1879. Dear Mothr. Mary said she promised to write to you a few lines on her return home. She got home one month ago today. We are all well. Our crops are good. We have one hundred an twenty five acres of land under the plow. I am some in debt. Probably one hundred dollars. I have some stock cattle and hogs. Mag and the little boys have to put the cattle on their ropes and change them from place to place and watter them which makes them a great deal of constant work. If I was able to fence eighty acres for a pasture I would be all right. I hope soon to be able. We are building a house 16 X 26 with an ell 14 X 20 one story under the ground, a basement, the ell for a cellar. The basement is rock on the basement. I will put a fraim 16 X 26 one story and a half on the ell one story giving us counting the cellar ten rooms. We have fifty peach trees with some fruit on each so that we are likely to have peaches enough to do us come good. Lyman has been very poorly all spring and sumer. Twenty one years old last may as you know. A big stout man with a strong tendency the doctor says to epilepcy. So I had to do a double portion of work so that that I am about played out. While I writeing Mary giving out to the little boys their spelling lesson. They spell well for their age and chance. Mary has Made a barrel of soap and washes bed cloths and made cloths for the little fellows. She has worked very hard since she came home. Nettie is about as big as her Mother. I got a letter from maggie Preshaw last winter stateing that the heirs thought that that N Y mony would be fourth comeing by the fourth of July. I would like to make a trip to Ill after a few hundred. I have not had any word direct from Homer for years so that I know nothing about him or his circumstances. I wish he would come up here. I supose that you nor Dick will ever come out here. This is a fine country. The improvement. I have about 5.000 black walnut trees groing from 1 to 4 feet high that will be valuable some day. Come and see us. Tell Dick to come. I will close by saying I am as ever your son. J.T.Stones

Mt Hope Aug 29, 1889. Dear Mother. I received you very wellcom letter in due and was glad to hear from you. I have not had a letter from Ill for many months. I have ofteen thought lately that I would soon hear that Death had again entered our family circle but had not thought that Aunt Longworth woul be the in the course of years the first to pass away but such is the mysteries of Providence. I have two Sundays this year preached two funerals each day before leaving our church. A thing I never did before in life. We are in good health now but I been in very poor health all summer for me. I thought last spring I come to Ill but cant on the account of failure of the wheat crop. We have not raised a bushel of wheat this year. We have plenty to live on and some to spare. I have not heard a work from Hoke for years. I do not know what has become of him. I would like to see him the best kind. I think Dick might come and see us. I remember that he has not written me a line sence I left Mo. Tell him to come out and see this country. I am breaking fast. My work is about done. A very few short years at most, like three or four. The last will tell the story with me. I anticipate the future tremblingly but the Judge of the whole earth will do wright. I submit my case into his hands. He knows I have tried to live right tho persoqatone? You say that the Estate will not be settled for two or three years yet. How does that happen. I had given it up in my mind years ago suposeing you had quit trying as I had not anything about it for years. I believe I have written all that would be of interest to you. I will close. Yours Truly J.T.Stones. write soon and often. Tell Dick to write. J T Stones. I have written to day to a friend in Colorado. (Envelope postmarked Red Coub Neb 31 Aug 1880 with a 3 cent stamp and addressed to Mrs. J. G. Stones McLean, McLean Co. Ill.)

Mt Hope Jan 30th 1881. Dear Mother. Your very wellcom letter allthough bearing sad news came to hand about two weeks ago. I should have answered before now but I got hurt about that time so I could not but am better now. We are all in common health now. Our little ones are going to school now. We are having a very hard winter. We are reasonably situated yeat times are hard. Money is scarce. I thought last winter I would come to see you then but I cannot with out sacrificeing more than I am able to loose. I hope I will be able to see you next fall.

Your letter is mostly made up of religious topics of which I am glad to hear but a coresponding answer I cannot give as those higher attainments I know nothing about them experimentally. Church matters in this part of the world is allmost a thing of the past. As you said of Aunt Eliza I think that those that have died right have made a very fortunate escape. I have not heard a word from Hok for years. I do not know where he is. If you do tell me whare is he and what are his circumstances. I think Dick might come out and make us a visit. Tell him to write. Mary wants you to tell her what has become of Betsy Bedows. What has become of her man Griffen. Whare does Betsy live. Tell Enos I think he might spend 5 cts in writeing to me. Have you had any late news from that N Y affair. If I had a little of it I would come to Ill. I have 160 acres of my land and got my government certificate. I expect to prove up on my other 160 in April 82. I am trying to get 160 for Lyman. Laura lives in less than 1 mile of us. I wish your health would permit you to come to see us. I have written untill I am getting tired so I will Close by subscribeing myself as ever. Yoour son. James T Stones. Direct to Red Coud as heretofore. Write soon.

Descendents

JT and Mary had nine children, five boys and four girls. Two boys and a girl passed away in childhood. A boy they named, William Tomes (probably Thomas) was born on November 1, 1866 and died November 20 when they were living in Eagleville, MO. Laura, Lyman and Nettie were born in Illinois. Margaret, Rolla and Zell were born in Missouri.

Laura married James Anderson and had a son, Jim Anderson and later married Bert Morris of Smith Center, Kansas and had a girl Mary Jenison and a son Vern Morris.

Lymon L married Margaret Francis and had sons James T and Thomas J and a daughter Hazel. James married Ester and had no children. Thomas married Gertrude Melva Myers and had Thelma Rose and Melva Henderson.

Nettie married Alonzo M. Francis and had one daughter Mary Effie (who married Frank Allen), and three sons, Carlos Olen (married Lulu Barbara Fitzgerald), Cyrus H. (named after his grand-father Cyrus Francis, died when he was 17) and James T. Francis (who never married).

Margaret married Andrew Upp and had Mary McCartney, Pearl Collins, boys Faye, Roy, Oral, Frank and Vivian Haresnape.

Rolla Hale married Leonia May Moler and had Belle Marie Myers, Mayme Berdine Rogers, George Hale and Glen Olin.

Zell Oliver married Mary Alice Francis and had Orbra Francis, Floyd Oliver, Cornelius Alonzo, Nettie Maye Wheeler, Ruth Ann McGinnis, and Loren Vern Stones.

Thomas H. Stones, youngest brother of J.T. Stones married Elvira Cunningham on Jan. 1, 1867. Two children were born of this union, Nell McFarland of McLean, Ill and Charles Stones of Haviland, KS. Nell had a son Paul and Charles had Marie, Dorothy, Charlotte and Virginia. Dorothy married Mr. McClung, a Hugoton, KS Pharmacist and Dorothy is the one who brought the letters from McLean, Ill.

The picture of Mt. Hope church is looking west from the northeast corner of the homestead with the cemetery on the left. JT donated the land from his homestead. The picture of the cemetery gate is on the east side. There is also an entrance on the north so that team and wagons or hearses could carry caskets to their plot. One picture shows Rev. J. T. Stones and the dates. It is a spire about six feet tall. Other pictures show his son Zell, grandson Cornelius and great grandson Norman's grave stones. Many other relatives are buried there. Great, great, grandson Martin has plots there too. The church has been rebuilt several times over the years.

Several years ago, a man by the name of Brown purchased the church and land other than the cemetery for one dollar and spent thousands to rehab the church and landscape the grounds. He had attended church there as a boy and had become wealthy in later life. It is referred to as a chapel now as church services are no longer held there as people have moved away.

The other sheets give information about his movement from Ohio to Illinois through Missouri and into Kansas. Letters written back to his mother in Illinois are included as he traveled from place to place. One picture is of me in about 1940 with my red wagon in front of the basement of the house that JT built. I was the last one born there. I still have the original homestead certificate number 3064 signed by President Rutherford B Hayes on November 1, 1880. It was filed on June 4, 1885 and signed by J. T. Stones. The land office was in Kirwin, Kansas.

Printed in the United States
By Bookmasters